IRAN'S DESTABILIZING ROLE IN THE MIDDLE EAST

HEARING

BEFORE THE

COMMITTEE ON FOREIGN AFFAIRS
HOUSE OF REPRESENTATIVES

ONE HUNDRED THIRTEENTH CONGRESS

SECOND SESSION

JULY 16, 2014

Serial No. 113–189

Printed for the use of the Committee on Foreign Affairs

Available via the World Wide Web: http://www.foreignaffairs.house.gov/ or
http://www.gpo.gov/fdsys/

U.S. GOVERNMENT PRINTING OFFICE

88–732PDF   WASHINGTON : 2014

For sale by the Superintendent of Documents, U.S. Government Printing Office
Internet: bookstore.gpo.gov   Phone: toll free (866) 512–1800; DC area (202) 512–1800
Fax: (202) 512–2104   Mail: Stop IDCC, Washington, DC 20402–0001

COMMITTEE ON FOREIGN AFFAIRS

EDWARD R. ROYCE, California, *Chairman*

CHRISTOPHER H. SMITH, New Jersey
ILEANA ROS-LEHTINEN, Florida
DANA ROHRABACHER, California
STEVE CHABOT, Ohio
JOE WILSON, South Carolina
MICHAEL T. McCAUL, Texas
TED POE, Texas
MATT SALMON, Arizona
TOM MARINO, Pennsylvania
JEFF DUNCAN, South Carolina
ADAM KINZINGER, Illinois
MO BROOKS, Alabama
TOM COTTON, Arkansas
PAUL COOK, California
GEORGE HOLDING, North Carolina
RANDY K. WEBER SR., Texas
SCOTT PERRY, Pennsylvania
STEVE STOCKMAN, Texas
RON DeSANTIS, Florida
DOUG COLLINS, Georgia
MARK MEADOWS, North Carolina
TED S. YOHO, Florida
SEAN DUFFY, Wisconsin
CURT CLAWSON, Florida

ELIOT L. ENGEL, New York
ENI F.H. FALEOMAVAEGA, American
 Samoa
BRAD SHERMAN, California
GREGORY W. MEEKS, New York
ALBIO SIRES, New Jersey
GERALD E. CONNOLLY, Virginia
THEODORE E. DEUTCH, Florida
BRIAN HIGGINS, New York
KAREN BASS, California
WILLIAM KEATING, Massachusetts
DAVID CICILLINE, Rhode Island
ALAN GRAYSON, Florida
JUAN VARGAS, California
BRADLEY S. SCHNEIDER, Illinois
JOSEPH P. KENNEDY III, Massachusetts
AMI BERA, California
ALAN S. LOWENTHAL, California
GRACE MENG, New York
LOIS FRANKEL, Florida
TULSI GABBARD, Hawaii
JOAQUIN CASTRO, Texas

AMY PORTER, *Chief of Staff*   THOMAS SHEEHY, *Staff Director*
JASON STEINBAUM, *Democratic Staff Director*

(II)

CONTENTS

IRAN'S DESTABILIZING ROLE IN THE MIDDLE EAST

WEDNESDAY, JULY 16, 2014

House of Representatives,
Committee on Foreign Affairs,
Washington, DC.

The committee met, pursuant to notice, at 10:08 a.m., in room 2172 Rayburn House Office Building, Hon. Ed Royce (chairman of the committee) presiding.

Chairman ROYCE. This morning we look at Iran's considerable efforts to destabilize the Middle East.

When it comes to Iran, attention has rightly been focused on efforts to stop its nuclear program. But as one witness will explain this morning, Iran's nuclear program is just the tip of the revolutionary sphere that extends across the world and threatens key U.S. interests. Iran's foreign policy, he goes on to say, is subversive, sectarian, and set on goals that would come at the expense of U.S. interests.

He is right. Indeed, with Iran's long support of terrorist groups and support of militias and adversarial regimes, the region has been feeling the brunt of this revolutionary sphere for quite some time. Thanks to Iran, Hamas has rearmed since 2012. Iran is the one that rearmed them, and nearly 80 percent of Israel's citizens are fleeing to bomb shelters this week as a result. With Iran's aid, Shi'a militias within Iran are rearming and they are mobilizing. The Assad regime, with the Iranian forces—with Quds Forces and with Hezbollah—continues to massacre Syrians. With Iran's aid, Hezbollah is able to threaten Israel with over 25,000 rockets and I can say that I saw some of this first hand. During the second Lebanon war I was on the ground in Haifa as those rockets were coming in. This was before the invention of the Iron Dome. There were 600 victims in the Rambam Trauma Hospital and they were targeting civilian neighborhoods, and Houthi rebels supported by Iran are closing in on Yemen's capital. That is quite a record for a regime now sitting across the table from us in Vienna where the administration has conceded that this number-one state sponsor of terrorism in the world can arguably enrich uranium. My concern is that they are conceiving that. I hope it is not conceiving it because that is the pathway to a nuclear weapon.

Of course, these aren't random efforts to support terrorism by the Iranian regime but concerted actions by this ayatollah-led—and he is the key decision maker—this Shi'a-led government to overturn what Iran believes is a regional power structure that favors the

(1)

United States, that favors Israel and their collaborators and when they say collaborators, of course, what they mean is the Sunni Muslim governments in the Gulf.

This is a recipe for disaster for the region. It is a recipe for U.S. interests there and today Iran's work is on full display as hundreds of rockets rain down on southern Israel. It is Iran that provides, again, the funding, the weapons, the training to Hamas and other Palestinian terror groups. Iranian leaders have admitted to providing the missile technology that Hamas used against Israel during the last Gaza conflict in November 2012, and just the other week a U.N. panel of experts concluded that rockets and weapons concealed on the Klos C including long-range M–302 rockets originated from Iran. Other shipments have gotten through as Hamas have fired the recently acquired rockets for the first time and, of course, those bring all of Israel within—or nearly all within range, certainly, Tel Aviv and Jerusalem. These weapons put 8 million people into Gaza's range of fire. One of them struck Hadera, a coastal city between Tel Aviv and Haifa, 73 miles north of Gaza.

In recent years, Iran has come under increasing strain from international sanctions aimed at stopping its nuclear program. This is what, frankly, got Iran to the table. When we talk about why they are at the negotiation table it is because of the sanctions passed here and adopted. But even with its economy damaged, Iran has managed to provide robust support to extremist proxies as part of its broader geopolitical agenda across the region. As one Ambassador from the region shared with me what do we think is going to happen if they come out from under those sanctions with respect to the capital that they will then have at their disposal for destabilization. Now the United States and other world powers are negotiating a final nuclear agreement with Iran that would lift most of the sanctions. Bad deal or good deal, and many of us fear a bad deal, any sanctions relief will bolster Iran.

As one witness notes, Iran stands to gain $100 billion in frozen bank accounts and billions as oil exports resume. That is a lot of M–302 rockets. How well an Iran unchained by international sanctions treat its neighbors—I hope how it treats its own citizens aren't an indication of how it is going to treat its neighbors. How are the United States and her allies positioned to counter Iran's destabilizing activities in the Middle East? I am afraid we are going to hear from one of our witnesses today not well.

And I will now turn to the ranking member for any opening comments that Mr. Engel of New York has.

Mr. ENGEL. Thank you very much, Mr. Chairman, and thank you for calling this timely hearing about Iran's destabilizing role in the Middle East.

As Iran continues waging its charm offensive with the international community, negotiating with the P5+1 over its nuclear weapons program, we cannot forget a basic fact: Iran remains the most active state sponsor of terrorism in the world and Iran is a key driver of regional instability.

From Syria and Iraq to Yemen and the Palestinian territories, understanding Iran's nefarious behavior is essential to protecting the interest of the United States and our allies.

Even as Iran's economy continues to falter under the weight of international sanctions, leaders in Tehran are plowing their scarce resources into elements of Iran's security apparatus that supports terrorism, particularly the Iranian Revolutionary Guard Corps and its Quds Force.

Iran also provides funding, weapons and other support to a wide range of terrorist groups including Hezbollah, Hamas, and Palestinian Islamic jihad. All of these groups have been designated as foreign terrorist organizations by the United States and we will continue to treat them as such no matter what happens in the nuclear negotiations.

I want to emphasize a point that you made in your opening statement, Mr. Chairman, with which I certainly agree and you and I have talked about this a great deal. It was sanctions that brought Iran to the negotiating table.

It was sanctions that made Iran think twice about moving forward and I don't think we should remove those sanctions for any situation that is not preventive of Iran being able to have a nuclear weapon.

I don't think we should willy nilly loosen sanctions on Iran. I think we should keep the sanctions until we see that they are dismantling their nuclear program.

Last week, Chairman Royce and I sent a bipartisan letter to President Obama signed by more than 340 House colleagues. That is more than three-quarters of the members of the House of Representatives. We asked the President to consult with Congress on the scope of any potential sanctions relief.

The letter noted that U.S. sanctions on Iran are based not only on its nuclear weapons program but also on Iran's ballistic missile program, its support for terrorism, its human rights abuses and its development of chemical and biological weapons.

Even if a comprehensive nuclear deal is reached, and it enjoys broad support on Capitol Hill, it is safe to say that Congress would not lift all sanctions on Iran unless it ceases to be a bad actor in the region and dramatically improve its behavior in all of these areas.

With hundreds of Hamas rockets raining down on Israel, we see the real impact of Iran's support for terrorism. In March, the Israeli navy intercepted the Klos C, a ship carrying Iranian rockets to the Gaza Strip including dozens of Syrian-produced long-range M–302 rockets which are capable of reaching high-density Israeli population centers such as Tel Aviv, Jerusalem, and Haifa.

By deliberately targeting civilian areas with these deadly weapons, Hamas is committing war crimes aided and abetted by Iran. I have to laugh at the crocodile tears coming out of Hamas terrorists in Gaza talking about the civilian population.

I think yesterday was an eye opener for many people when the Egyptian-brokered cease fire was accepted by Israel but rejected by Hamas. It is clear to see who wants peace and who refuses to want peace.

And Hamas would not and could not be so bold without all the support it has received from Iran. Iran, again, is the number-one supporter of terrorism around the world and Hamas is a terrorist organization.

So in almost every conflict in the region we see Iranian finger-prints as Tehran seeks to spread its influence and manipulate its neighbors.

Iran's support for Assad in Syria and for Hezbollah's intervention in the Syrian civil war has given the regime a new lease on life and resulted in the deaths of thousands of innocent Syrian civilians.

Assad would not be winning, potentially, in Syria if it wasn't for Hezbollah, a terrorist organization supported, funded, maintained, and controlled by Iran. Iran's support for Hezbollah has also destabilized Lebanon and allowed the terrorist group to amass tens of thousands of rockets on Israel's northern border.

Iran's involvement with the Maliki government and with radical Shi'a militias in Iraq have undermined efforts to establish a more inclusive government in Baghdad.

So I don't think the U.S. should be cooperating with Iran on the situation in Iraq and I was pleased to hear Secretary Hagel's remarks last week confirming that we are not doing so.

So Mr. Chairman, in conclusion, let me say at this time of great instability in the Middle East we need to remain clear-eyed about the capabilities and intentions of our adversaries, especially Iran.

I look forward to hearing the testimony of our distinguished panel of witnesses and thank you again for holding this important and timely hearing.

Chairman ROYCE. Thank you, Mr. Engel. We now go to Ms. Ileana Ros-Lehtinen, chair of the Middle East Subcommittee.

Ms. ROS-LEHTINEN. Thank you so much, Mr. Chairman. While the administration takes unilateral steps to offer concessions to Iran as it pursues a weak nuclear agreement, it continues to disregard our calls for congressional oversight and our warnings on dealing with Iran while ignoring its destabilizing efforts.

The regime in Tehran continues to actively and openly work against U.S. national security interests across the globe in Iraq and Syria. It arms and finances terrorist groups like Hezbollah and Hamas.

Ted Deutch and I just came back from a trip to the region and many leaders expressed to us that pushing back Iran's breakout capability is not as important as dismantling Iran's nuclear infrastructure would be.

Iran doesn't need the bomb to be dangerous. Just having the capability to get the bomb is enough to spark a nuclear arms race in the region.

Instead of offering concessions to the regime, the administration should be pressing Iran to dismantle completely its nuclear program; abandon its support for Assad and its terrorist proxies; and cease its provocations against the U.S. and our ally, the democratic Jewish state of Israel, or else we will impose even stricter sanctions that will bring Iran's economy to its knees. It is the sanctions, stupid.

Thank you, Mr. Chairman.

Chairman ROYCE. Thank you, and we appreciate you and Mr. Ted Deutch's recent trip to the Middle East. Mr. Deutch is the ranking member of the Middle East Subcommittee. We will go to Ted Deutch for 1 minute.

Mr. DEUTCH. Thank you, Mr. Chairman. Thank you, Ranking Member Engel, for holding today's hearing and for your continued leadership and attention to Iran not just on the nuclear issue but to the whole of Iran's habitual bad behavior.

We are just days away from seeing whether Iran is truly committed to finding a diplomatic solution to the nuclear crisis. But even if there is a diplomatic resolution to Iran's ongoing quest for a nuclear weapon, it would not change the fact that Iran would still be the largest sponsor of terrorism in the world, it would still be assisting the Assad regime in Syria, and it would still be repressing the basic human rights of its citizens.

I would caution those who think that if a nuclear deal is reached that the world will simply ignore Iran's other violations of international norms including its meddling in regional affairs and attempts to incite instability in other countries.

In the more likely scenario that a nuclear deal with Iran is not reached or if the duration of the deal is not long enough, an Iranian regime that still possesses the capability of developing a nuclear weapon would surely set off a nuclear arms race in the region.

Mr. Chairman, we will know a lot more about Iran's intentions in the coming days. We must also be making our intentions clear—deal or no deal. The U.S. will not turn a blind eye to Iran's attempts to exploit a volatile Middle East.

I appreciate it and I yield back.

Chairman ROYCE. Thank you, Mr. Deutch. Mr. Brad Sherman of California is the ranking member on the Terrorism, Nonproliferation, and Trade Subcommittee.

Mr. SHERMAN. Iran is the number-one state sponsor of terror. Hezbollah, Assad—a reach that included the Buenos Aires Jewish Community Center, a point on the globe as far from Tehran as one can get.

Now imagine an Iran with the impunity of being a nuclear weapons state. But we should realize that we have limited bargaining power. We do not have Iran's economy completely on the ropes.

We did not adopt sanctions that were effective 10 or 15 years ago. We did it 10 or 15 months ago. We brought them to the table but we have not brought them to their knees unless we can imagine Iran with no centrifuges, no terrorism, and no theocracy.

But I don't know whether we have rallied public opinion to the point where we are willing to, for just an example, ban Chinese imports to the United States as long as Japan maintains—or China or any other country maintains an economic relationship with Iran. That is the level of sanctions that I think goes beyond what we can adopt here in Washington.

We are wise to have this hearing to illustrate to Americans and Europeans why it is so important that all options remain on the table. I yield back.

Chairman ROYCE. Thank you, Mr. Chairman.

This morning we are pleased to be joined by a distinguished group of experts on this subject. Dr. Ray Takeyh is senior fellow for Middle East studies at the Council on Foreign Relations.

Mr. Takeyh was previously a senior advisor on Iran at the Department of State. He was professor at the National Defense University.

We also have Scott Modell, a senior associate at the Center for Strategic and International Studies. He serves as a senior advisor to U.S. Special Operations Command on counter threat finance issues. He was previously a senior officer in the National Clandestine Service at the Central Intelligence Agency.

And Dr. Natan Sachs—Natan, as he is known, is currently a fellow at the Brookings Institution's Center for Middle East Policy. Previously, Dr. Sachs was a fellow at Stanford Center on Democracy Development and Rule of Law and a Fulbright Fellow in Indonesia.

So without objection, these witnesses' full prepared statements will be part of the record. We are going to encourage them to summarize and then we will go to questions. Members will have 5 calendar days to submit statements and questions and anything extraneous for the record.

Dr. Takeyh, if you would like to begin.

STATEMENT OF MR. RAY TAKEYH, SENIOR FELLOW FOR MIDDLE EASTERN STUDIES, MIDDLE EAST PROGRAM, COUNCIL ON FOREIGN RELATIONS

Mr. TAKEYH. Thank you, Mr. Chairman. It is a privilege for me to be here again as well as with my colleagues Scott and Natan.

I will just briefly discuss some aspects of my testimony. I think the high drama of arms control negotiations and diplomacy in Vienna today dominates our impressions of Iran and defines those.

In the next couple of weeks the diplomats will debate how much centrifuges are to be traded for how much sanctions relief. There is already talk that negotiations may be extended past July 20th, given the significant gaps that remain between the two powers.

The nature of the inspection regime and enforcement mechanism will also be discussed. Whether a durable agreement can be negotiated with an unreliable partner, as you suggested, such as the Islamic Republic, will be put to a test.

Hovering over all these technical issues is the challenge of addressing Iranian revisionism in the era of nuclear diplomacy. Tehran, as was mentioned, is busy advancing its claims in a contested Middle East, and Washington would be wise to check the surge of Iranian power and negate its regional designs.

The key actors defining Iran's regional policy are not urbane diplomats mingling with their counterparts in Europe but the Revolutionary Guards, particularly the famed Quds Brigade. For the commander of the Quds Brigade, General Qassem Suleimani, the struggle to evict America from the Middle East began in Iraq and now has moved to Syria.

Syria is the front line of that particular resistance. For the hardliners in Iran, the Sunni state's attempt to dislodge Bashar Assad from power is really a means of weakening Iran.

The survival and success of the Assad dynasty today is a central element of Iran's foreign policy. Next door, Iran's model of operation in Iraq actually draws from its experiences in Lebanon in the early 1980s when Iran essentially amalgamated various Shi'i parties into a lethal Hezbollah organization and Hezbollah has remained the instrument of Iran's foreign policy since then.

Since the removal of Saddam, Iran has similarly been busy strengthening Shi'i forces in Iraq by subsidizing their political activities and arming their militias. Iran hopes that Shi'ites will continue to exploit their demographic majority to solidify their political gains.

But should the political process fail, they must be sufficiently armed to win the civil war. The purpose of Iran military dispatches to Iraq initially were to evict the United States and now it is to maintain the viability of Shi'a forces.

A certain misapprehension, I think, was born in Kabul and has migrated to Baghdad, mainly that we need Iranian assistance to stabilize our war-torn charges. The ISIS surge in Iraq is once more portrayed as an opportunity for the two powers—United States and Iran—to collaborate.

The stark reality remains that United States launched Iraq with much sacrifice on this path of precarious stability despite Iran's harmful interventions and to do so again will require American initiative rather than Iranian benevolence.

Iran's fundamental interest in Iraq tends to diverge from those of the United States. We ostensibly seek an inclusive Iraq with greater participation of Sunni forces in the Shi'i government.

Iran desires a Shi'i hegemony with the veneer of Sunni participation. Iran essentially desires an Iraq that is estranged from the Arab Councils and at odds with the United States.

Today, as you mentioned, the region is feared and gripped with fear that arms control policy will lead to a larger detente between the United States and Iran. This concern has some justification in history during the heydays of arms limitation talks between the United States and the Soviet Union.

Nuclear accords were often followed by commerce and diplomatic recognition. Washington has often been seduced by the notion that nuclear agreement can pave the way for other areas of cooperation.

The challenge that the United States faces today is to defy its own history. America must find a way to impose limits on Iran's nuclear ambitions through negotiations while restraining its regional ambitions through pressure.

This will require rehabilitation of America's battered alliances in the Middle East. Strategic dialogues and military sales are not going to be sufficient. Washington can reclaim its allies' confidence but it cannot do so without being an active participant in Syria and Iraqi sagas.

Further attempt to exempt ourself from this conflict will mean that our pleasures will ring hollow to a sceptical Arab audience. Thank you, Mr. Chairman.

[The prepared statement of Mr. Takeyh follows:]

COUNCIL *on*
FOREIGN
RELATIONS

1777 F Street, NW, Washington, DC 20006
tel 202.509.8400 fax 202.509.8490 www.cfr.org

Iran's Destabilizing Role in the Middle East

Prepared Statement by

Ray Takeyh

Senior Fellow for Middle East Studies, Council on Foreign Relations

Before the Foreign Affairs Committee
United States House of Representatives
July 16, 2014.

The high drama of arms control negotiations in Vienna dominates the headlines and defines impressions of Iran. Diplomats will debate how many centrifuges are to be traded for how much sanctions relief. The nature of inspection regime and enforcement measures are all said to be sorted out this week. Whether a durable agreement can be negotiated with an unreliable partner such as the Islamic Republic will be put to a test. Hovering over all the technical issues is the challenge of addressing Iranian revisionism in the era of nuclear diplomacy. Tehran is busy advancing its claims in a contested Middle East, and Washington would be wise to check the surge of Iranian power and negate its regional designs.

The Islamic revolution of 1979 left a permanent imprint on Iran's foreign policy orientation. Ayatollah Ruhollah Khomeini bequeathed his successors an internationalist vision that divides the world between the oppressed and the oppressor. Such a view is consistent with Shia political traditions where a minority sect struggled under Sunni Arab rulers that were often repressive and harsh. Thus, the notion of tyranny and suffering has a powerful symbolic aspect as well as practical importance. Iran is not merely a nation seeking independence and autonomy within the prevailing order. The Islamic revolution was a struggle between good and evil, a battle waged for moral redemption and genuine emancipation from the cultural and political tentacles of a profane and iniquitous West. Irrespective of changing nature of its presidents, Iran will persist with its revolutionary and populist approach to regional politics.

For much of the past three decades, the Islamic Republic's inflammatory rhetoric and aggressive posture concealed the reality of its strategic loneliness. Iran is, after all, a Persian nation surrounded by Arab states who were suspicious of its revolution and its proclaimed objectives. The Gulf sheikdoms arrayed themselves behind the American shield, Iraq sustained its animosity toward Iran long after the end of its war, and the incumbent Sunni republics maintained a steady belligerence. Iran nurtured its lethal Hezbollah protégé and aided Palestinian rejectionist groups but appeared hemmed in by the wall of Arab hostility. All this changed when Iraq was reclaimed by the Shias and the Arab Spring shook the foundations of the Sunni order. Today, the guardians of the Islamic Republic see a unique opportunity to project their power in a region beset by unpredictable transitions.

For Ayatollah Ali Khamenei Arab Spring means "a people have emerged who are not dependent on America." Whatever confidence-building measures his diplomats might be negotiating in Vienna, the Supreme Leader insists that Iran is "challenging the influence of America in the region and it is extending its own influence." In Khamenei's depiction, America is a crestfallen imperial state hastily retreating from the region. Whatever compunctions Tehran may have had about American power greatly diminished with the spectacle over Syria where Washington's redlines were erased with the same carelessness that they were initially drawn.

The key actors defining Iran's regional policy are not its urbane diplomats mingling with their Western counterparts in Europe, but the Revolutionary Guards, particularly the famed Quds Brigade. For the commander of the Quds Brigade, General Qassim Soleimani the struggle to evict America from the region began in Iraq. "After the fall of Saddam, there was talk by various individuals that they should manage Iraq, but with Iraq's religious leaders and Iran's influence, America could not reach that goal," proclaimed Soleimani. The struggle moved on and today "Syria is the front-line of resistance." For the hardliners, the Sunni states attempt to dislodge Bashar Assad is really a means of weakening Iran. The survival and success of the Assad Dynasty is now a central element of Iran's foreign policy.

The fear gripping Arab capitals is that an arms control agreement will inevitably lead to détente with Iran. This concern has some justification in history. During the heydays of arms limitation talks between the United States and the Soviet Union, nuclear accords were often followed by commerce and diplomatic normalization. Washington has often been seduced by the notion that a nuclear agreement can pave the way for other areas of cooperation. The challenge for the United States is to defy its own history. America must find a way to impose limits on Iran's nuclear ambitions through negotiations while restraining its regional ambitions through pressure. This will require rehabilitation of America's battered alliance system in the Middle East. Strategic dialogues and military sales can only go so far. Washington's cannot reclaim its allies' confidence without being an active player in Syria and Iraq. So long as America exempts itself from these conflicts, its pledges will ring hollow to a skeptical Arab audience.

Syria: The Touchstone of Middle East Politics

The Arab Spring and its promises of peaceful democratic change grounded to a halt in Syria. Bashar Assad followed the grisly footsteps of his father in massacring his countrymen. The civil war in Syria is not just tearing up that hapless country but it is defining the future of the region. The Middle East is a region that perennially divides against itself. The late Malcom Kerr, one the preeminent historians of the region, once described the 1960s as a time of an Arab cold war with the monarchies and radical republics struggling against each other. Power more so than ideology defined that cold war, thus allowing it to gradually fade. Today, a different and a more durable cold war is descending on the Middle East, this time underpinned by sectarian identities. Syria is at the heart of this conflict, pitting Iran and the Shia militants against Saudi Arabia and the Sunni sector. The region cannot regain its footing unless the Syrian civil war somehow ends.

In the heady days of the Arab Spring, despots were collapsing with alacrity that heartened even the most cynical observers of the Middle East. A region known for authoritarian stability was suddenly faced with mass protests and calls for democratization that were proving successful. "Assad must go" was proclaimed from the seat of Western chancelleries. How could he not go when the more formidable House of Mubarak collapsed with such ease? And how could the President of the United States not call for the departure of an adversary after he had called for the eviction of America's most trusted ally when he faced a popular revolt.

Still, Syria proved different. Its divided ethnicities, its central role in Iran's assault on the prevailing Arab order, meant that Assad had many more cards up his sleeves. Washington proclaimed a goal but failed to plan for the actual removal of Assad. It is difficult to predict with precision how a civil war unfolds. By their very nature, civil wars are unpredictable phenomena, subject to sudden shifts and changing fortunes. However, it is not too premature to suggest that the morale of Assad forces is high while the fragmented opposition is suffering from lack of arms and the absence of international patronage. The infusion of Russian arms, Iranian funds and Hezbollah troops will ensure that Assad is well-maintained. The opposition can add to this misfortune the image of Syria's tyrant begin accredited by the United Nations for dismantling chemical weapons he was not supposed to have, much less use.

The Islamic Republic's calculations always differed from those of the United States. The mullahs were confident that Assad could turn back the tide of history. To check Iran's power in the Levant, the United States has to an active player in Syria. By providing arms to reliable rebels, taking a firm stand against Russian and Iranian mischief, it is still possible to dislodge Assad from power. This challenge becomes more difficult every day. Too many lives have already been lost and too much advantage has already been ceded to Assad and the Ayatollahs. The reversal of this trend will prove a formidable but ultimately a necessary task.

Iraq Comes Undone

As the Islamic Republic contemplates its policy in Iraq, it has to content with a number of difficult positions. Tehran's overriding objective is to prevent Iraq from once more emerging as a dominant power in the Persian Gulf. Thus, it is critical for the theocratic regime to ensure the Shia's political primacy. However, Iran must also guard against any spillover from the enraging civil war that is threatening Iraq's territorial cohesion. Dismemberment of Iraq into three fledgling states at odds with each other would present Iran with more instability in its immediate neighborhood. To pursue its competing goals, Iran has embraced a contradictory policy of pushing for elections and accommodating responsible Sunni elements while at the same time subsidizing Shia militias who are bend on violence and disorder.

Iran's model of operation in Iraq is drawn from its experiences in Lebanon in the early 1980s. At that time, Iran amalgamated a variety of Shia parties into the lethal Hezbollah. Since the removal of Saddam, Iran has similarly been busy strengthening Shia forces by subsidizing their political activities and arming their militias. Iran hopes that the Shias will continue to exploit their demographic advantage to solidify their gains. But should the political process fail, they must be sufficiently armed to win the civil war. The purpose of Iran's military dispatches was initially to evict the United States from Iraq and now it is to maintain the viability of Shia forces.

A certain misapprehension was born in Kabul and has migrated to Baghdad, namely that we need Iran's assistance to stabilize our war-torn charges. The ISIS surge in Iraq is once more portrayed as an opportunity for the two powers to collaborate. The stark reality remains that we launched Iraq on its path of precarious stability despite Iran's harmful interventions. And to do so again will require American initiative and not Iranian benevolence. To successfully combat Iran's regional influence, the Iraqi government must be pressured into limiting the scope of Iran's intrusions and denying their mischievous neighbor privileged sanctuaries.

America's Role.

Although the United States has been effective in estranging Iran from its European allies, we have played a limited role in affecting Iran's position in the Middle East. Beyond arms sales to Arab states and attempts to assuage Israeli concerns, we have not undertaken a systematic effort to isolate Iran in its immediate neighborhood. To succeed in limiting Iran's reach, all of its regional assets have to be contested. From the Shia slums of Baghdad to the luxurious palaces of the Gulf, Iran has to find a new, inhospitable reality as it searches for partners and collaborators.

The success of America's Iran policy to some extent hinges on the nature of U.S.-Israeli alliance. Simply put, Iran today pointedly dismisses the possibility of U.S. military retaliation irrespective of its provocations. It is entirely possible that Iranians are once more misjudging America's predilections. Nonetheless, while America's military option has receded in the Iranian imagination, Israel still looms large. Fulminations aside, Iranian leaders take Israeli threats seriously and are at pains to assert their retaliatory options. It is here that the shape and tone of U.S.-Israeli alliance matters most. Should the clerical regime sense divisions in that alliance, they can assure themselves that a beleaguered Israel cannot possibly strike Iran while at odds with its superpower patron. Such perceptions cheapen Israeli deterrence and diminish the potency of the West's remaining sticks.

All this is not to suggest that Washington cannot criticize Israeli policies, even publicly and forcefully. The ebbs and flows of the peace process will cause disagreements between the two allies. But, as it plots strategies for easing tensions between Israel and is neighbors, the administration would be wise to insist that the dynamics of Israeli-Palestinian relations will not affect Washington's cooperation with Israel on Iran.

Despite all professions of common interests and subtle and indirect hints of cooperation to come, the Islamic Republic will only alter the dimensions of its foreign relations if it is confronted with a dramatic threat. As in 2003, Khamenei will be prone to pay a high price for his survival. Should we gain sufficient coercive leverage then we will be in a position to alter Iran's policies. Under these circumstances, we would impose important and durable restraints on Iran's nuclear program. Iran would be asked to cease subverting its neighbors and limit its support to Hezbollah and Hamas to political advocacy. Human rights would have to assume a high place in our negotiations—Iran must be pressed to honor international norms on treatment of its citizens. In the end, it is important to stress that the confrontation between the United States and Iran is a conflict between a superpower and a third-rate autocracy. We should not settle for trading carrots and sticks and hoping for signs of elusive moderation from truculent theocrats. A determined policy of pressure can still ensure that the Islamic Republic will be a crestfallen, endangered and therefore a constructive interlocutor.

———————

Chairman ROYCE. Thank you, Doctor.

STATEMENT OF MR. SCOTT MODELL, SENIOR ASSOCIATE, BURKE CHAIR IN STRATEGY, CENTER FOR STRATEGIC AND INTERNATIONAL STUDIES

Mr. MODELL. Chairman Royce, members of the committee, thank you very much for the opportunity to come here today. You have read my testimony. I think everybody is sort of in agreement with what I have summarized in my testimony.

There are a few points I wanted to extract from it, expand a bit on it and one was the idea that I think has been encapsulated in some of the initial comments was basically that Iran, beyond the nuclear program, approaches its revolutionary agenda in a whole of government approach.

There is a lot of talk here in the United States about how we do things around the world, you know, sort of incorporating a whole of government approach currently working in the Pentagon and a lot of our time is spent trying to figure out how do we bring together State Department and a variety of agencies to accomplish certain foreign policy objectives overseas and it is not easy.

But if you look at what Iran does from bottom up in terms of trying to project their power and trying to accomplish their agenda throughout the Middle East they really do take a whole of government approach, certainly more so than the Arab States that I have seen.

The nuclear deal, I think, one of the things that I am continuously seeing and hearing that really surprises me is the fact that people are going to—that they are considering giving a pass on the possible military dimensions of the program. I hope that is inaccurate. We have been watching this for over a decade and it is almost astonishing that that could be ignored.

So in the run-up to a deal and discussions between the administration and Congress on the implementation of a long-term deal I really hope that that is addressed.

I also agree with the chairman that I think the revolutionary agenda is going to go on. Years ago I recall in 2011 and 2012 members of the Basij who were posted, you know, into Syria and Iraq and elsewhere there were several public interviews and they were asking them what they thought about Iran's agenda in the region.

And this was—these were public interviews and they were—and they said well, we have—our agenda is to create a million-man force across the entire region.

They recently said that again—they are interested in making a 200,000-man force that is going to spread from Iran all the way to Lebanon. I think there is a lot of obstacles in the way of doing that but the core objective remains true and you can see they are pushing on that objective constantly.

The other thing I would say is, just because Iran is involved in P5+1 talks and has been for some time, I think there is a quick rush to assume that the proliferation activities have stopped. I think in the run-up to an agreement or in the aftermath of an agreement people are going to start wondering what is this inspection and verification regime going to look like.

And I would posit to you the most—one of the most important aspects of it has to be how do we devise a new containment strategy with our allies in the region, not only with the IAEA inside looking at facilities to ensure they are not cheating and abiding by the terms of the agreement but it is the external part that they have built up and done such a good job over the last decade that contributes to proliferation and has allowed them to move their program so far forward.

When we start to think about how we are going to work together with the GCC more effectively in the future and develop a new containment strategy we have to have that in mind and I have recommended a number of ways in which we should start thinking about how the U.S. Government should be using resources overseas to that end in my paper.

Thank you.

[The prepared statement of Mr. Modell follows:]

"Iran's Destabilizing Role in the Middle East"

Prepared testimony of Scott Modell, Senior Associate,
Center for Strategic and International Studies (CSIS)
Before the House of Representatives Committee on Foreign Affairs

July 16, 2014

Chairman Royce, Members of the Committee, good morning and thank you for this opportunity to testify on Iran's Destabilizing Role in the Middle East. I will briefly describe the "Iran Action Network," Iran's long-term foreign policy goals and how they destabilize the region, and current trends, and offer recommendations on how to counter one of our most pressing national security challenges.

Introduction

U.S. policy toward Iran has focused mainly on addressing the nuclear challenge, but it has overlooked the threat posed by Iran's global revolutionary network. The U.S. nuclear strategy, which is based on the dual pillars of sanctions and diplomacy, is realistically grounded, well-resourced, and run about as effectively as can be expected. However, Iran's nuclear program is just the tip of a revolutionary spear that extends across the world and threatens key U.S. interests. Iran's foreign policy is subversive, sectarian, and set on goals that would come at the expense of U.S. interest in the region.

For more than three decades, Iran has sought to preserve the Islamic revolution at home and promote it abroad, through a network of government and nongovernment organizations that I have referred to as the Iran Action Network (IAN). The members of that network are involved in crafting and implementing the covert elements of Iran's foreign policy agenda, from terrorism, political, economic and social subversion; to illicit finance, weapons and narcotics trafficking; and nuclear procurement and proliferation.

The Iran Action Network

Iran relies primarily on three organizations to coordinate and oversee IAN activities:

- The Qods Force, an elite branch of the Islamic Revolutionary Guard Corps, responsible for irregular warfare and asymmetric operations, including a wide range of subversive activities from non-violent cultural and business fronts to direct support to political resistance organizations and violent opposition groups.
- The Ministry of Intelligence and Security (MOIS) is Iran's primary civilian intelligence agency. It has the lead role in foreign intelligence collection and several covert action programs, both at home and abroad. It works closely with all of Iran's closest proxies in the region and second only to the Qods Force in Iran's global efforts to export the Islamic Revolution.
- Lebanese Hezbollah has been Iran's strongest non-state ally since its inception in 1982. While Hezbollah's role in projecting Iranian power has traditionally been tied to the goals of

fighting Israel and protecting Lebanon, it remains a key element in fighting on the front lines in Syria, alongside Qods Force advisors and trainers and Syrian army units.

In short, the IAN is Iran's "whole-of-government" approach to preserving the regime at home and coordinating and promoting the revolution internationally. Its actions encompass a remarkable array of covert action, including covert influence operations, sanctions evasion, terrorism, training and equipping Islamic militants, and other so-called "resistance activities."

A Destabilizing Foreign Policy

U.S. policy toward Iran has focused mainly on addressing the nuclear challenge, but it has overlooked the threat posed by Iran's global revolutionary network. Based on the dual pillars of sanctions and diplomacy, the U.S. nuclear strategy is realistically grounded, well- resourced and run about as effectively as can be expected. However, Iran's nuclear program is just the tip of a revolutionary spear that extends across the world and that threatens key U.S. interests.

Today, Iran is hoping to cut a nuclear deal that will bring its economy back online. A revived economy is precisely what Iran needs to jump start operations in the Levant, Yemen, Afghanistan, and across the region, that have slowed down significantly due to shrinking operational budgets. Even in an environment of fiscal austerity, Iran continues to pursue a foreign policy agenda that has destabilizing effects on the region, to include the following:

- West Bank and Gaza: Iran continues to provide arms, funds, intelligence, and training to Palestinian terrorist groups, most notably, Hamas and Palestinian Islamic Jihad. Both groups oppose the existence of Israel and commit acts of terrorism to that end.
- Lebanon: Iran's closest non-state ally is Lebanese Hezbollah, long considered one of the world's most dangerous terrorist organizations. Iranian force projection around the world depends on Hezbollah operatives and networks, from the front lines in Syria to criminal safe havens in West Africa.
- Syria: Iran's military intervention in Syria turned the tide of the war and prevented the collapse of the Assad regime. By siding with Assad, Iran has inflamed sectarian divisions across the region, leading to an unprecedented flow of Sunni foreign fighters into Syria and surrounding countries.
- Iraq: Iran has sought to ensure that either Maliki or other pro-Iran Shiite politicians remain in control of Iraq. To counter the spread of the Islamic State, Iran is expanding Shia militia groups such as Kata'ib Hezbollah and Asaib Ahl al-Haq that operate under Iran's direction beyond the control of the Iraqi government.
- Bahrain: Iran continues to support Bahraini Shiite dissident groups that seek to overthrow the Bahraini monarchy and replace it with an Islamic republic similar to Iran. Bahraini security officials continue to see signs of Iranian support to local IED attacks.
- Saudi Arabia: Hezbollah of the Hejaz carried out attacks in Saudi Arabia, including the 1996 Khobar Towers bombing in Dhahran. Iran continues to stir up Shia dissident groups in eastern Saudi Arabia, and Saudi leaders generally recognize Iran as a subversive force in Syria, Lebanon, and on Saudi borders in Yemen.
- Yemen: Iran has supplied arms, funds, and probably intelligence to Houthi rebels. Along with Sudan, Yemen has become the center of Iran's regional platform for covert arms production and distribution. African ports, increasingly seen as effective transshipment point by transnational crime organizations, serve Iran's objectives elsewhere in the region.

- Afghanistan: Iran has consistently balanced its support for the government in Kabul with material support to the Taliban and the Haqqani Network. IAN-controlled networks on both sides of the Iran-Afghan border facilitate the illegal flow of men, money, and materiel.

Current Trends

First, a nuclear agreement with Iran will give a much-needed boost to the Iranian economy. By most accounts, Iran stands to gain access to nearly $100 billion dollars frozen in foreign banks, as well as billions more as oil export restrictions are lifted. At the same time, several EU countries appear poised to return to Iranian markets, adding billions of dollars more in potential foreign direct investment and trade. All of this will provide the leaders of the IAN with the resources they need to gradually return to previous levels of operational activity. It means funding proxies that were either cut off or cut back due to sanctions; reassessing the ongoing closure or downsizing of Iranian embassies in non-traditional areas such as Latin America; expanding joint military training and security programs in Africa; and increasing funding for Hamas, PIJ, and the new Palestinian coalition government.

Second, several countries in the Gulf should expect to see a resumption of covert activity, including training, weapons, and non-lethal support to local proxies, especially in Bahrain, Kuwait, and Saudi Arabia, where Iran has a history of supporting Shia opposition movements. The GCC countries will also have to confront the growing threats posed by Iran in the area of Computer Network Exploitation operations. Iranian hackers employed primarily by the MOIS target the computer systems of U.S. and Gulf personnel, companies, and government facilities. Iran has treated past Stuxnet attacks on centrifuges at Natanz as a declaration of cyber war, and is now responding in kind.

Third, IRGC Qods Force commander Qasem Soleimani will find ways of increasing military support to the Assad regime. Keeping Assad in power will remain a strategic priority, mainly because it strengthens Iran's relationship with its most important partner in the region, Lebanese Hezbollah, but also because in Iran's eyes there is no alternative. Soleimani will also be focused on countering the growth of Sunni extremism in Iraq, which has reached levels of violence unseen since 2007. He will probably offer to increase current initiatives that arm, train, and fund new and existing pro-Iranian Shia militants in Iraq. Soleimani has more say over what Iran does in Syria and Iraq than President Rouhani, enjoying the full support of the Supreme Leader. His number one priority will remain building an arc of influence and power across the Levant, often referred to as Iran's "Shia crescent."

Fourth, there are few signs that a nuclear Iran will increase the chances of a near-term nuclear arms race in the Middle East. U.S.-GCC bilateral security relationships have evolved for more than 25 years. Any strategic shift away from the United States would take years given the depth of the commitments involved. GCC countries are rightfully more concerned about Iran's attempts to exploit the very real issues of religious extremism, demographic pressures, and other internal sources of instability that each Gulf state is trying to address on its own.

Fifth, Iran has gone to considerable lengths to create a global shadow apparatus designed to evade sanctions. It enables the Iranian government to support Islamic movements and pro-Iran militants around the world and spread the value of the "resistance" via cultural, social, economic, political, and business entities and organizations. That apparatus goes hand in hand with the asymmetrical nature of almost everything Iran does. The international community needs to develop a better understanding of this apparatus for several reasons, but largely because it is directly linked to some of Iran's most destabilizing activities.

Sixth, as long as a nuclear deal does not address Iran's ballistic missile program, which appears to be the case given outright rejection of the idea by the Supreme Leader, Iran will continue to develop long-range ballistic missiles can strike any target in the GCC and add further to its arsenal of short-range artillery rockets that can strike coastal areas across the Gulf. Iran will attempt to improve the accuracy of its missiles and rockets, and pursue the indigenous production of UCAVs, cruise missiles, and possibly even nuclear warheads.

The Way Forward

Even if sanctions and diplomacy lead to a nuclear agreement with Iran, the activities of the IAN will continue to pose significant obstacles to Iran's diplomatic outreach to the Gulf and the West. In some cases, lethal support to Shia opposition groups across the region also threatens both U.S. and international security. To address these threats, policymakers should consider the following recommendations:

- **Coordinate U.S. Efforts Against Networks.** U.S. policymakers should call for an interagency and international task force for developing and deploying a comprehensive and global campaign against the operational and strategic depth of the IAN. Such a task force would target the illicit networks and operatives associated with the Iran Threat Network, including its financial, business, and logistical support networks. The goal should be a counter network disruption campaign, modeled where appropriate, on previous successful U.S. whole-of-government initiatives against defiant state actors that combine overt and covert action, law enforcement, sanctions, and containment.
- **Refine and Expand Soft War Initiatives.** The Supreme Leader repeatedly refers to the U.S.-led "soft war" as the single biggest threat to the existence of the Islamic Republic. An effective soft war should expose and neutralize the state and non-state actors involved in subversive activities that are instrumental in marketing the Islamic Revolution overseas. At the very least, this should include Qods Force, MOIS, and Hezbollah operations and criminal activities. Of equal importance are Iran's non-official cover organizations – religious, cultural, and charitable – as well as businesses that effectively blur the lines between overt and covert activity.
- **Focus Efforts on Transnational Organized Crime.** In addition to being one of the world's most formidable terrorist and paramilitary organizations, Hezbollah has become involved in a global criminal enterprise involving money laundering, racketeering, and drug trafficking. Indicting Hezbollah as a transnational criminal organization would dispel its image as an elite and "pure" resistance organization. We should approach and counter Hezbollah from the vantage point of strategic law enforcement, financial sanctions, and even the International Court of Criminal Justice (for its long record of global terrorism, for its involvement in the assassination of a democratically elected head of state, and possibly even for war crimes being perpetrated in Syria).
- **Developing Non-Military Policy Options.** At any given time, dozens of U.S. government agencies are pursuing the same elements of the IAN. To improve the way multiple agencies work against the IAN, the government has to be better organized. In relatively new and developing areas such as Counter Threat Finance, it would go a long way to work from an agreed-upon "financial order of battle" that maps key networks on a transnational scale (e.g.,

banks, exchange houses, front companies, trade-based money laundering, shipping companies, etc.). In doing so, U.S. government agencies should draw assiduously on partner country liaison services as part of a global effort to build a coalition of like-minded states. An order of battle would generate a series of non-military or military-enabled policy options that could serve as the basis of a strategic intelligence and law enforcement campaign – not just a series of strikes.

- **Focus on Counter Threat Facilitation.** As long as Iran has an agenda of creating new centers of power in the world and doing so at the expense of the United States, it behooves us to consider a law enforcement-led "Counter Threat Facilitation" initiative. Such an initiative should emphasize strategically planned law enforcement operations to expose illicit networks, arrest their perpetrators, freeze assets and attack the IAN's crime-terror pipelines though the international trade and banking system. It could go a long way in weakening the illicit financial networks around the world that buttress Iran's strategic foundations, revolutionary resolve, domestic staying power, and power projection capabilities.

- **Create Offices of Irregular Warfare.** As sanctions are eased, the U.S. government will need to find other ways of identifying and disrupting Iran's involvement in nuclear proliferation, terrorism, and other threats to international security. If sanctions and military options make way for other policy options, the U.S. will have a much more difficult time identifying and countering many of the IAN's illicit activities, which tend to be irregular or asymmetric in nature. Creating offices of irregular warfare in various government agencies would go a long way toward exposing and damaging the criminal foundations of the IAN. While irregular warfare is usually the domain of the military, several operationally robust and aggressive non-kinetic initiatives should be considered. In the area of Information Operations, for example, covert influence authorities "with teeth" are necessary to more effectively bolster Iranian moderates in Iran and to undermine Iran's message to audiences in Africa, Central Asia, and across the Middle East. In the still developing area of Counter Threat Finance, the Treasury Department should be put on a financial and economic warfare footing, or better integrated with interagency partners who possess the needed level of financial operational authorities and capabilities. Treasury needs to be more involved in financial operations, particularly overseas, where there are significant gaps of understanding in the areas of international banking and finance. Finally, the U.S. cannot do it alone. The IAN has grown increasingly transnational, making it critical to have the support of foreign liaison partners who have the ability to hit Iran's threat facilitation networks (transport, shipping agents, freight forwarders, warehouses, pilots, airlines, etc.). Properly incentivizing our partners to conduct higher impact operations against the IAN depends on creativity, money, and persistence. The Rewards for Justice Program, or a version thereof, should offer payouts to exceptional foreign government officials or units who successfully assist U.S. government initiatives.

Conclusion

With or without a nuclear deal, the strategic calculus of the Supreme Leader and much of the ruling conservative establishment is the same today as it was when the Islamic Revolution began: preserve the regime at home and deter threats from abroad, while externalizing the revolution and resistance. The IAN is the engine of the regime and will resume Iran's pursuit of broader goals in the region. Look for a return to past levels of activity by elements of the IAN, including units of the Qods Force, whose budgets have been cut back as a result of Iran's economic downturn. This means more operations in Syria, where Iran will continue to work closely with the Assad regime and Iran-trained, equipped, and guided militant networks; further attempts to support Shia activism in Bahrain, where Iran has attempted several times to create the conditions for regime change; continued use of Iraq as a transit point for illicit commerce coming from the Gulf, and the movement of men, money, and illicit materiel across the Levant; deeper support to Hezbollah and the newly-formed Palestinian coalition government; and likely increases in training, weapons, and funding to the Houthi rebels in Yemen and pariah states such as the Sudan.

GCC countries will continue to harbor deep suspicion, distrust, and enmity toward Iran, well aware of Iran's unrelenting efforts to create internal dissent and destabilization through support to local Shia opposition movements. Still, they will refrain from pursuing their own nuclear programs (other than the UAE) and continue to rely instead on strong bilateral security partnerships with the United States. For its part, Iran will push Hezbollah to do some of its more complicated bidding in Arab countries, which Hezbollah sometimes agrees to, other times not. Finally, the peaceful intentions of a nuclear Iran will take decades to validate. Until that happens, expect more denial, deception, and dissimulation from the IAN.

Chairman ROYCE. Thank you.
Dr. Sachs.

STATEMENT OF NATAN B. SACHS, PH.D., FELLOW, SABAN CENTER FOR MIDDLE EAST POLICY, THE BROOKINGS INSTITUTION

Mr. SACHS. Thank you very much, Chairman Royce, Ranking Member Engel, distinguished members and staff for the opportunity and honor of speaking here today, especially alongside Ray and Scott.

I will speak briefly about Israeli views of this issue. While there is considerable good will in Israel toward the Iranian people, the Islamic Republic's regime is viewed very differently, and with good reason. Indeed, virtually no one in Israel, including those who strive in earnest for peace with their Arab neighbors, expects good relations with the Islamic Republic as currently constituted. Nonetheless, important, though limited, variation exists among Israeli policy makers on the regional challenges posed by the Iranian regime.

In my testimony I will touch briefly on the spectrum of Israeli views on two such regional challenges—Iran's nuclear program and its involvement in terrorism and conflicts abroad.

In my written testimony I elaborate further on these issues and discuss the related question of an alliance of interest between Israel and Saudi Arabia and Iran's nuclear program.

It is important to note first that far more unites Israelis on the Iranian nuclear issue than divides them. Diversity of opinion exists but the spectrum of opinions is narrow and much more limited than on other issues, such as the Israeli-Palestinian conflict. Virtually no one in Israel's national security elite, nor for that matter in the U.S., doubts Iran's intention to reach threshold nuclear capabilities.

Israeli experts and, indeed, the government do not contend that Iran has already decided to build a nuclear weapon but they do not doubt that Iran intends to have the capability to do so.

Further, almost all in Israel view the possibility of a nuclear threshold Iran as a very negative development, for a variety of reasons. Most mainstream thinkers support the need to project a credible threat to stop Iran's nuclear program if all else fails, even by means of conventional force.

And yet, there remain meaningful differences among mainstream Israeli thinkers. First, not all view the Iranian nuclear threat with equal severity or use the term ''existential threat'' to describe it.

Some even argue that even if all failed, Israel will be strong enough to deter a nuclear Iran. Most people abroad believe Israel has a second strike capability—notably, Iran believes this.

Iranian acquisition of nuclear weapons might then entail a grim but perhaps stable cold war logic of mutually assured destruction. This debate rests, of course, on a related debate about Iran's rationality, which I will be happy to discuss if asked to.

Second, there is an important variation among senior Israeli thinkers on what might constitute an acceptable deal with Iran. Some central figures have suggested that very low levels of uranium enrichment coupled with stringent inspection might leave enough time to react to an Iranian breach of an agreement.

Third and perhaps most dramatically, there are different views in Israel on the wisdom of a unilateral strike on Iran's nuclear facilities. The Israeli cabinet and security forces have been strongly divided on the issue and former security officials have warned publicly against a unilateral strike.

Polling suggests that the Israeli public too is divided on the issue and is skeptical of a unilateral strike without U.S. support, and I stress that point. Note that there is considerable difference and tension between the need to project readiness to strike if all else fails, something which nearly all Israelis support, and actual support for a strike, on which opinion diverges.

While the credible threat of a strike could help the diplomatic track, its credibility can be undermined when these differences emerge publicly, as they have.

In sum, on the threat of Iran's nuclear program, far more unites Israelis than divides them but some differences exist on the extreme severity of a threat, the nuances of remedies, and on the wisdom of unilateral strike.

By comparison, there is very little debate in Israel on Iran's involvement in conflicts and in terrorism in the region and abroad. In the past, there was some debate over the degree of Iran's control over Hezbollah, its most significant subsidiary abroad.

Some argue that Hezbollah should be viewed more as a Lebanese party than an Iranian proxy. The civil war in Syria has largely ended that debate in Israel. At Tehran's behest, Hezbollah has sacrificed greatly in casualties and in sinking popularity among Arab and Lebanese publics, and yet it has done so.

Beyond the immediate region, Hezbollah, along with the Iranian Revolutionary Guard, also carried the threat of global terrorism against Israeli and even non-Israeli targets, most famously, the bombing of the Jewish Community Center in Buenos Aires— AMIA—20 years ago this very week.

A special concern to Israel—at this very moment—is also Iran's involvement with militant Palestinian groups, most notably the Palestinian Islamic Jihad, or PIJ—a close Iranian subsidiary and a very violent terrorist group.

Hamas' relationship with Iran is more complex. Unlike PIJ, Hamas is a large political party as well as a terrorist organization. Hamas is also an offshoot of the Muslim Brotherhood and its relation with Shi'a Iran and with Assad's regime in Syria, once robust, have soured.

Nonetheless, Iran and Syria have been suppliers of weapons for militants in the Gaza Strip including Hamas. Syria-produced M–302 rockets, as you mentioned, Mr. Chairman, for example, have been used against Israeli civilians in the past week.

Let me conclude by noting a key concern of all Israeli policy makers of the full spectrum I described. Israelis fear that, should a deal with Iran be reached, whether before July 20th or after an extension, there will be some in the international community who will view the issue as closed—the nuclear issue and other issues.

In reality, the success of any deal will depend completely on the monitoring and verification embedded in it. Israelis are therefore likely to continue to focus on this issue.

U.S. interests, which are aligned with, though not identical to those of Israel, would be well served if the United States too maintained a vigilant, pragmatic but realistic watch over Iran's policies in the future.

Thank you very much, Mr. Chairman.

[The prepared statement of Mr. Sachs follows:]

Israel and Iran's Role in the Middle East

Prepared Testimony before the hearing of the House Committee on Foreign Affairs, 113th U.S. Congress, on "Iran's Destabilizing Role in the Middle East"

July 16, 2014

Natan B. Sachs

Fellow, Center for Middle East Policy at the Brookings Institution

Chairman Royce, Ranking Member Engel, distinguished members of the committee and staff, thank you for the opportunity and the honor of testifying today. It is a special pleasure to testify alongside such distinguished scholars.

Few regimes evoke such strong concern, among so many different countries, as does the Islamic Republic of Iran. Israel is, of course, among the most concerned, and its government views dealing with Iran's nuclear program as its most important national security issue, bar none.

The open animosity and covert hostilities between the two countries are relatively new. Unlike Israel's longstanding disputes with several of its Arab neighbors, Iran and Israel had a close relationship before the Iranian Revolution. Between Israel and Iran lie two other countries and vast swaths of desert, and in many respects their fundamental interest are complimentary. Indeed, before the revolution, Iran was viewed by Israeli national security thinkers as part of a "periphery doctrine" in which Israel allied itself with non-Arab actors in the Middle East, to counterbalance its dramatic inferiority in numbers and, then, in wealth, compared to the Arab countries that surrounded it.

Today, too, one can often hear among Israelis an appreciation for the Iranian people and a genuine desire for better relations between the peoples of the two countries. The scars of the long Arab-Israeli conflict do not, by and large, apply to Iran directly; despite politics, there is considerable goodwill in Israel toward Iranians as people.

But the Islamic Republic, the regime that governs Iran, is viewed very differently by Israelis of all walks of life, and with good reason. Virulently anti-Israeli, the Islamic Republic's leaders have frequently referred to Israel as the "Little Satan" accompanying the "Great Satan," the United States. Iranian leaders have made Israel a feature of their public statements.

In part, this anti-Israeli posture helps remedy the Iranian regime's inherent public relations problem, as a Shi'a theocracy, in the largely Sunni Muslim world. By rhetorically confronting the perceived enemy of many Muslims, Iran can gain a place of honor among them. Such was the case, in the past, with the Lebanese Hizballah, Iran's protégé, which by fighting Israel gained legitimacy among many who would otherwise oppose it as a sectarian and theocratic Shi'a movement in multi-ethnic Lebanon. More importantly, the Iranian regime has backed its rhetoric with a long track record of stoking violence against Israel and even against Jewish targets worldwide, often through proxies such as Hizballah.

As a result, virtually no one in Israel, including those who strive in earnest for peace with Israel's Arab neighbors, expects a true rapprochement between the Islamic Republic, as currently constituted, and Israel in the near or medium-term future.

Nonetheless, important—though limited—variation does exist among Israeli policymakers on the challenges posed by the Iranian regime and on what Israel might do to counter them. In the remainder of my testimony, I will touch on two different aspects of Iran's role in the Middle East and on mainstream Israeli views with regard to them: the narrow but meaningful spectrum of opinions within the Israeli national security elite about Iran's nuclear program; and Iran's involvement in terrorism and conventional conflicts against Israel and around the world. I will conclude with some remarks on the limited, but real, potential for an alliance of convenience between Israel and another major adversary of Iran's current regime, the Kingdom of Saudi Arabia.

Iran's Nuclear Program

There are meaningful differences among mainstream Israeli thinkers about how to deal with Iran's nuclear program, as I will discuss, but it is important to note first that far more unites Israelis on this issue than divides them. Diversity of opinion, in other words, exists, but the spectrum is narrow and the variation small. Let me begin by describing the main points about which Israelis are largely unanimous, before describing the important differences that remain.

First, virtually no one in Israel's national security elite, nor, for that matter, in the U.S. government or among the P5+1 countries, doubts Iran's intention to reach threshold nuclear capabilities. The simultaneous pursuit of extensive uranium enrichment capabilities, far beyond anything needed for civilian purposes, a separate plutonium track, efforts at developing weaponization technology and delivery systems, all coupled with repeated Iranian efforts at subterfuge and concealment of its nuclear program, leave no doubt among Israelis about Iran's intention to develop nuclear weapons capabilities.

Israeli experts, and indeed the Israeli government, do not contend that Iran has already decided to build a nuclear weapon, but hardly any among them doubt that Iran intends to have the capability to do so if it so chooses in the future.

Second, almost all in the Israeli national security community view the possibility of a nuclear-threshold Iran as a very negative development. A nuclear threshold Iran could act as a catalyst for nuclear proliferation in the highly volatile Middle East. Nuclear threshold capabilities might also embolden Iran in other, conventional involvements in the region. While not all Israelis agree on the severity of this threat, as I will discuss, virtually no one dismisses it offhand.

Third, clearly most Israeli policymakers support the need for keeping "all options on the table" and for projecting a credible threat to stop Iran's nuclear program by use of Israeli conventional force, if necessary. As I will discuss, there are considerable differences among Israelis in their views of when and how force might be used and how readily Israel should use it unilaterally, but nearly all view an Israeli ability to act as an important complement to the diplomatic track led by the United States and other major world powers.

And yet, there are meaningful differences among mainstream Israeli thinkers and even among recent heads of security agencies. First, while all Israelis view the Iranian nuclear program with deep concern, not all view the threat with equal severity. The often used term "existential threat", in particular, is not used by all to describe the Iranian program. Even if Iran were to decide to "break out" of a threshold posture and acquire a weapon, some argue, Israel would be strong enough to deter it effectively.[1]

Though, undoubtedly, a nuclear power, with effective delivery systems, could devastate Israel, a very small country, the threat is mitigated by the second strike capabilities that most believe Israel possesses. Most importantly, the Iranian regime itself believes Israel is a nuclear

---

[1] For examples, see Ari Shavit, "Former Mossad Chief: An Attack on Iran Likely to Foment a Generations-long War," *Ha'aretz*, September 1, 2012, http://www.haaretz.com/weekend/magazine/former-mossad-chief-an-attack-on-iran-likely-to-foment-a-generations-long-war-1.461760; as well as: "Report: Barak Says Iran is Not Existential Threat to Israel," *Ha'aretz*, September 17, 2009, http://www.haaretz.com/news/report-barak-says-iran-is-not-existential-threat-to-israel-1.7710

power with such second strike capabilities. A reality in which Iran has acquired nuclear weapons would then entail a grim but perhaps stable, cold-war logic of mutual assured destruction (MAD), which might deter Iran from ever using a weapon.

This debate rests on a related debate, that of Iran's rationality. [2] While the Islamic Republic's goals are clearly different than what would seem reasonable to most Americans or Israelis, their rationality in *pursuing* these goals is another matter. Clearly sophisticated and calculated, Iranian leaders would know the potential ramifications of an overt—and ascribable—nuclear attack on Israel. Given that the regime likely views its own survival as a primary concern, the likelihood of such an overt attack is diminished.

There exists, of course, the possibility of a less overt attack, should Iran acquire nuclear weapons. With several terrorist organizations working closely with Iran, it is at least possible that nuclear weapons could be transferred and used by an individual or group other than the Islamic Republic itself. Though possible, and very worrisome given the stakes, this remains a long-shot in most views.

Several Israelis have also pointed to the unnecessary demoralizing aspect of depicting Iran as an existential threat.[3] Describing a nuclear Iran in this way would present ordinary Israelis with a seemingly impossible dilemma. It would give Israelis the false perception that if all fails and Iran were to acquire nuclear capabilities, their country is doomed. Many in the Israeli elite, and among its diplomats, therefore prefer to avoid this term.

Second, there is important variation among senior Israeli security thinkers on what might constitute an acceptable deal, from Israel's perspective, between the P5+1 countries and Iran. All agree on the importance of dealing with Iran's plutonium track as well as the importance of the weaponization aspects of Iran's program, but there are nuances on the levels of residual Uranium enrichment Iran might be permitted. While the Israeli government has made clear its position that no enrichment capabilities in Iran would be acceptable, some important voices in Israel have suggested that very low levels of enrichment, coupled with stringent inspection, might leave the international community, and Israel, enough time to react to a breach of an agreement.[4] The key, as always, is in the details: how long the remaining "break out" time would be; how stringent the inspections would be over time; and what advancement in Iranian enrichment technology would be possible in the meantime.

Third, and perhaps most dramatically, there are different views in Israel on the wisdom of a unilateral Israeli strike on Iran's nuclear facilities, and on the timing of such a strike, should it be ordered. Multiple reports, and my own interviews, suggest that between 2010 and 2012 the Israeli cabinet was strongly divided on the issue, with several ministers and chiefs of intelligence

[2] "'Irrational' Iran Can't Get Nuclear Arms: Netanyahu," *Reuters*, July 11, 2010, http://www.reuters.com/article/2010/07/11/us-nuclear-iran-netanyahu-idUSTRE66A1FI20100711; Chemi Shalev, "Netanyahu: 'I won't wait until it's too late' to decide on Israeli Attack on Iran," *Ha'aretz*, July 14, 2013, http://www.haaretz.com/news/diplomacy-defense/.premium-1.535724#!.

[3] Barak Ravid, "Mossad Chief: Nuclear Iran Not Necessarily Existential Threat to Israel," *Ha'aretz*, December 29, 2011, http://www.haaretz.com/print-edition/news/mossad-chief-nuclear-iran-not-necessarily-existential-threat-to-israel-1.404227.

[4] Amos Yadlin and Avner Golov, "The United States, Israel, and the Possibility of Formulating an Outline for a Final Agreement with Iran," INSS Insight, No. 543, (April 30, 2014), http://d26e8pvoto2x3r.cloudfront.net/uploadImages/systemFiles/No.%20543%20-%20Amos%20and%20Avner%20for%20web043254200.pdf.

and the military advising caution and restraint, while the prime minister and minister of defense held more hawkish views on the matter. Since then, former security officials involved in the debates have criticized the prime minister openly on this issue.[5]

Public opinion polling suggests that the Israeli public, too, is divided on the issue of a strike on Iran's nuclear facilities.[6] Like many Israeli policymakers, the public seems especially attune to whether a strike would be led by the United States—in which case the public, though apprehensive, might well support Israeli involvement—or whether Israel would act on its own—in which case the public is far more skeptical of the merits of a strike. While the Israeli leadership has devoted a great deal of effort and resources to secure an Israeli capability to act alone—and the United States, and the U.S. Congress in particular, have done a great deal to help in this effort—there are those in Israel who believe a unilateral strike might not be worth the considerable risks.

Note that there is a considerable difference and tension between the need to project readiness to strike if all else fails—something which nearly all Israelis support—and actual support for a unilateral strike, on which opinions diverge. While the credible *threat* of a strike could help the diplomatic track, and might even be essential to successful diplomacy, its credibility can be undermined when these differences emerge publicly.

Fourth, there is some debate in Israel on the strong and vocal focus on the Iranian nuclear threat exhibited by the current government of Israel. Even the current chief of the Mossad, Israel's foreign intelligence service —who answers directly to the prime minister and who is heavily tasked with the Iranian file—recently noted that the unresolved conflict with the Palestinians, rather than Iran, poses a graver long-term threat to Israel.[7] Others frequently argue in private that the public focus on Iran has given the damaging impression of a purely Israeli-Iranian confrontation over the Islamic Republic's nuclear program rather than, more appropriately, an issue between the international community and Iran.

However, others contend, and with reason, that the Israeli diplomatic focus on Iran's nuclear program has created the sufficient urgency in the international community to deal with the issue seriously, from an extensive sanctions regime to robust diplomacy. Ehud Barak, the former Israeli minister of defense, when deflecting criticism of his and Prime Minister Benjamin Netanyahu's approach, noted the success of Israel's effort to place Iran's nuclear program at the top of the international agenda. He lamented the damage done to Israel's international effort by the internal discord on the matter.[8]

In sum, on the threat of the Iranian nuclear program, far more unites Israelis than divides them. But some differences exist among Israelis on the extreme severity of the threat, the nuances of the remedies that might be acceptable in a diplomatic agreement on the program, on

---

[5] Natan Sachs, "Israel's Spy Revolt," *Foreign Policy*, May 10, 2012, http://www.foreignpolicy.com/articles/2012/05/10/israels_spy_revolt.

[6] See Shibley Telhami, "The February 2012 Israeli Public Opinion Survey," The Brookings Institution, February 29, 2012, http://www.brookings.edu/research/reports/2012/02/29-israel-poll-telhami.

[7] Barak Ravid, "Mossad Chief: Palestinian Conflict Top Threat to Israel's Security, Not Iran," *Ha'aretz*, July 5, 2014, http://www.haaretz.com/news/diplomacy-defense/.premium-1.603249#!.

[8] Shlomo Cesana and Matti Tuchfeld (in Hebrew) "*Barak: "Havurat Olmert Poga'at BeMa'amad Yisrael"*" (Barak: The Olmert Gang Damages Israel's Standing) *Yisrael Hayom*, May 3, 2012 http://www.israelhayom.co.il/site/newsletter_article.php?id=16698&hp=1&newsletter=03.05.2012.

the wisdom of a unilateral Israeli strike on Iran's nuclear facilities, and on the seemingly singular and vocal diplomatic focus on the Iranian nuclear issue.

Iranian Involvement in Conflicts Abroad

Where there is particularly little debate among Israeli policymakers and analysts is on the involvement of the Islamic Republic in conflicts abroad. From Israel's perspective, Iran's influence can be felt most strongly in Lebanon, through its proxy, the Lebanese Hizballah, in terrorism abroad against Israeli and even non-Israeli Jewish targets, and in assistance to militant Palestinian groups, most notably to the Palestinian Islamic Jihad (PIJ), to smaller splinter Islamist groups and, to a lesser degree, to Hamas.[9]

Hizballah

The strongest and most significant of the Iran-sponsored groups is Hizballah, the "Party of God," established in 1982. As a Shi'a militia, Hizballah focused both on a fight against Israel, which was embroiled in a lengthy war in Lebanon starting in June 1982, and against other factions in the intricate Lebanese political scene. Hizballah, it should be remembered, has not only been involved in fighting and in terrorist attacks against Israel; The Shi'a Lebanese organization was also directly involved in the bombing of the U.S. Marine barracks in Beirut in 1983.

In the past, there was some debate in Israel over the degree of control of Iran over Hizballah. Some argued that Hizballah was, first and foremost, a Lebanese organization that would not sacrifice its position in Lebanon for Iran's needs. As I've heard from senior Israeli officials, the civil war in Syria has ended that debate in Israeli circles. At Tehran's behest, Hizballah has become involved heavily in the sectarian Syrian civil war on the side of the Assad regime, sustaining significant casualties and greatly diminishing its standing among ordinary— and usually Sunni—Arabs, as well as among most of the Lebanese people. This sacrifice by Hizballah provides strong evidence of its deference toward Tehran.

Hizballah's involvement in Syria has left it exposed in Lebanon, and therefore perhaps less inclined to stoke conflict with Israel at the moment. But in the longer term, the Hizballah and Iranian involvement in Syria has helped prop up the Assad regime and secure the Syrian conduit of materiel from Iran to Hizballah. Although Israel and Hizballah have maintained a strained quiet since 2006, born of deterrence wrought in the Israeli "Second Lebanon War" against Hizballah, the organization remains a major concern for Israeli policymakers. Israel views Hizballah as a persistent threat both on its own, and in any possible future confrontation between Israel and Iran.

---

[9] See Fares Akram, "In Gaza, Iran Finds An Ally More Agreeable Than Hamas," *The New York Times*, July 31, 2013, http://www.nytimes.com/2013/08/01/world/middleeast/in-gaza-iran-finds-a-closer-ally-than-hamas.html; Jonathan Schanzer and Grant Rumley, "Iran Spawns New Jihadist Group in Gaza," *The Long War Journal*, June 28, 2014,
http://www.longwarjournal.org/archives/2014/06/by_jonathan_schanzer.php?utm_source=rss&utm_medium=rss&utm_campaign=iran-spawns-new-jihadist-group-in-gaza#.

International Terrorism

Of further concern to Israel is the robust and long standing involvement of Iran, and especially of the Iranian Revolutionary Guard Corps (IRGC) and of Hizballah, with Iranian support, in international terrorism against Israeli targets abroad.

Some of these attacks, including in Delhi, Tbilisi and Bangkok, should be viewed in the context of a long covert war between Israel and Iran, mostly surrounding Iran's nuclear program.[10] In Iranian eyes, perhaps, attacks on Israeli diplomats are retribution for the assassinations of Iranian nuclear scientists, for which Iran blames Israel. Other attacks however, have little to do with this ongoing covert war.

Most horrifically, Iranian sponsored terrorism has hit overtly civilian targets abroad, including non-Israeli Jewish targets. These include, famously, the bombing of the Jewish Community Center in Buenos Aires (AMIA) twenty years ago this week, which killed 85 people. Israeli intelligence has long contended that Iran was complicit in the terrorist attack; last year the Argentinean special prosecutor for the case released a lengthy report to similar effect.[11]

Support for Palestinian Militants

Of special concern to Israel is also Iran's involvement with militant Palestinian groups, which have inflicted misery on both Israelis and Palestinians, and have consistently undermined the Israeli-Palestinian peace process. PIJ, in particular, has served as an Iranian subsidiary, carrying out deadly terrorist attacks at Iran's command, including suicide attacks. In 1995 in Beit Lid, in Israel, a PIJ operative blew himself up among Israeli soldiers. A second suicide terrorist waited for rescue teams to arrive before detonating his own device and killing both survivors of the first blast and rescuers who rushed to their aid. PIJ operations contributed significantly to undermining the Oslo Process in its early years and weakening support among Israelis for the Rabin government's efforts at peacemaking. In subsequent years, PIJ has continued this deadly pattern against Israeli civilians on numerous occasions.

Hamas's relationship with Iran is more complex. Unlike PIJ, Hamas is a large political party as well as a militia involved in terrorism. Hamas is also an offshoot of the Muslim Brotherhood, a Sunni Islamist organization. As such, there are limits to the alignment between Shi'a Islamist Iran and Sunni Islamist Hamas in the recent context of the sectarian conflict engulfing the Middle East. Hamas's political leadership has had to leave Damascus, in light of the Syrian civil war and the widespread animosity between Sunni Islamists across the Middle East and the Iranian-backed Syrian regime; Relations with Tehran, once robust, have soured accordingly.

Nonetheless, the shared animosity toward Israel allows for strange alliances. Iran and Syria have been important suppliers of weapons for militants in the Gaza Strip, including Hamas.

---

[10] Ethan Bronner "Israel Says Iran Is Behind Bombs", *The New York Times*, February 13, 2012, http://www.nytimes.com/2012/02/14/world/middleeast/israeli-embassy-officials-attacked-in-india-and-georgia.html?pagewanted=all;
Thomas Fuller "Israeli Envoy Links Bangkok Bombs to Attacks in India and Georgia", *The New York Times*, February 15, 2012, http://www.nytimes.com/2012/02/16/world/asia/bombs-in-bangkok-linked-to-india-and-georgia-attacks-israeli-envoy-says.html

[11] http://www.nytimes.com/2013/05/30/world/americas/prosecutor-in-argentina-says-iran-plotted-with-hezbollah-in-latin-america.html?_r=0

Syrian-produced M-302 rockets, for example, have been used against Israeli civilians in the current round of fighting. The same type of rockets were found on the KLOS C arms ship, which the Israeli navy intercepted before it could reach Gaza. The KLOS C originated in the Iranian port of Bandar Abbas.[12]

Following the Egyptian military's recent action against most of the tunnels that connected northern Sinai and the Gaza Strip, the opportunity for weapons smuggling has diminished significantly. This offers some hope that the supply of weapons, Iranian and other, will be more difficult after the conclusion of this round of fighting, "Operation Protective Edge" in the Israeli terminology.

Nonetheless, the long and bloody track record of the IRGC, Hizballah, PIJ, and Hamas, suggest that Iranian involvement in fomenting anti-Israeli terrorism in Israel, in the West Bank and Gaza Strip, and abroad, are likely to continue in a variety of forms.

An Alignment of Interests between Israel and Saudi Arabia

The Islamic Republic has acquired an array of adversaries, in part due to its robust and widespread efforts at fomenting instability outside its borders. This, in and of itself, suggests an opportunity for its adversaries to align.

The regional context is important in this regard. With a broad sectarian conflict sweeping the Middle East, Sunni and Shi'a powers find themselves at odds. This confrontation exacerbates the longstanding rivalry between Saudi Arabia and Iran, in particular.

The events of the past three years have also created a rift between, on the one hand, traditional Arab powers such as Saudi Arabia and, now, Egypt, and on the other hand, those perceived to be more closely aligned with the Muslim Brotherhood, such as Qatar and Turkey.

The result is that Israel and some of the traditional Arab powers now have aligned interests, with shared conflicts with both the Islamic Republic of Iran and its allies, and with Muslim Brotherhood organizations such as Hamas. Indeed, on Iran's nuclear program in particular, Israel and Saudi Arabia share many views.

This alignment has even had a public aspect to it, with a public meeting of former intelligence chiefs from Israel and Saudi Arabia, Amos Yadlin and Turki bin Faisal Al Saud, respectively.[13] Both former officials remain influential in their countries and their meeting was likely coordinated with the current authorities.

And yet, a few words of caution are in order. First, the origins of the rivalry between Israel and Iran are very different than those between Iran and Saudi Arabia. Saudi Arabia and Iran each view themselves as the rightful leaders of Sunni and Shi'a Islam, respectively; they both straddle the Persian (or "Arabian") Gulf; Saudi Arabia has a sizeable Shi'a minority in the

---

[12] Lazar Berman and AFP, "40 Missiles, 181 Mortars, 400K Bullets Found on Arms Ship," *The Times of Israel*, March 9, 2014, http://www.timesofisrael.com/40-missiles-181-mortars-400k-bullets-found-on-arms-ship/; Yaakov Lappin, "Syrian-made M302 Rocket Fired by Hamas at Hadera," *The Jerusalem Post*, July 9, 2014, http://www.jpost.com/Operation-Protective-Edge/Syrian-made-M302-rocket-fired-by-Hamas-at-Hadera-362008.

[13] See "Israel and the Middle East: Seeking Common Ground, A Conversation with HRH Prince Turki bin Faisal Al Saud and General Amos Yadlin," The German Marshall Fund, May 26, 2014, http://www.gmfus.org/israel-and-the-middle-east-seeking-common-ground/.

eastern part of the country, where much of its oil is found; and the two countries have long vied for prominence in their immediate vicinity. Added to this is the horrific civil war in Syria, which has Sunni militias of a variety of stripes, some of whom have Saudi support, fighting against the Iran-backed Assad regime.

In short, the Saudi-Iran confrontation is deeply rooted not only in the Islamic Republic's behavior, but in the geopolitical positions and aspirations of the two countries. It is not merely Iran's policies that worry Saudi Arabia, in other words, but Iranian power itself.

Israel, on the other hand, has little issue with Iran as such. The grave Israeli concerns over Iran relate directly to the policies of the Islamic Republic. Israel, like Saudi Arabia is gravely concerned with Iran's nuclear program and with Iran's activity outside its borders; but unlike Saudi Arabia, Israel has little interest in the Sunni-Shi'a divide that defines much of the fighting in the Middle East today. In practical terms, this means that Israel has deliberately avoided siding with either of the warring factions in Syria, focusing instead only on preventing the transfer of advanced weaponry to Hizballah. In other words, Israel's interests, unlike Saudi interests, dictate focusing on particular aspects of Iran's activity in the region, even while avoiding others.

All this suggests that while there is room for cooperation between Saudi Arabia and Israel, this alignment of interests is necessarily shallow and contingent on interests that may change over time or context.

Moreover, the public meeting of the former officials of the two countries was striking precisely because the optics of this relationship are highly sensitive. Arab public opinion remains deeply hostile to Israel and acutely sensitive to the Palestinian cause. The persistent Palestinian-Israeli conflict, currently at an especially low point, hinders the ability of Saudi Arabia and Israel to pursue an alliance fully.

****

This week will see the planned deadline for negotiations between the P5+1 and Iran on the Iranian nuclear program. Whether or not a deal is reached—now or after an extension—the issue of Iran's nuclear program will not disappear.

A key concern of Israeli policymakers is that, should a deal be reached, there will be some in the international community who will view the issue as closed. In reality, the success of any deal will depend completely on the monitoring and verification embedded in it. Israelis are therefore likely to continue to focus on this issue. Their concerns will be amplified by Iran's continued destabilizing role in several countries in the Middle East and among Palestinian militant groups, as well its extensive involvement in terrorism abroad.

These grave concerns over the Islamic Republic of Iran's policies, though not without debate in Israel, are, as a rule, shared across the Israeli national security community. U.S. interests, which are aligned with—though not identical to—those of Israel, would be well served if the United States too maintained a vigilant, pragmatic but realistic watch over Iran's policies in the future.

Chairman ROYCE. We appreciate your testimony. Thank you, Mr. Sachs.

We go now to a question that I have for Mr. Modell and this goes to your testimony that by most accounts you say Iran stands to gain access to nearly $100 billion in frozen banks as well as billions more as oil export restrictions are lifted as part of any agreement, whether that agreement is good or bad. That is the consequence.

Could you translate that impact of this relief—what that would mean? What operational capabilities do you estimate the Iranians could develop or acquire as a result of the release of this funding?

Mr. MODELL. Mr. Chairman, sure. One of the reasons why the tempo of Iran's operational activity over the last year or so since sanctions kicked in in earnest has been exactly that. They haven't had the funding to fund all of their units.

They haven't had the funding to do certain things, just as if— the same way with the U.S. Government or any government, for that matter.

In times of financial crisis there are certain things you got to cut back and certain things you can't. In the case of Iran with a surplus—with an influx of $100 billion plus bringing back oil online, the IRGC ghost force becomes much more active.

Funding that goes to proxies in the region goes back up to pre-sanctions levels and you start to see more activity in places like Yemen. You start to see more activity in places further outside their normal operating areas in the Middle East.

They have had to cut back activities in Latin America and Africa and other places because of the sanctions. Those activities will pick up, particularly on the covert side, in my opinion.

Chairman ROYCE. So the added advantage that what they might perceive as a windfall what would that give the regime specifically in the region?

If you were just to look at the Middle East, sort of the low-level insurrection that they support in Saudi Arabia and some of these other—among the Shi'a population there and some of the other developments; could you maybe specify what that would mean?

Mr. MODELL. One of the things that I would say is what they have been trying to do for a long time now and they did this, and Dr. Takeyh had mentioned this, in the 80s they had a number of Hezbollah movements outside of Lebanon. They tried to replicate the example of Lebanese Hezbollah in Bahrain and Hezbollah Hejab in Saudi Arabia and so forth.

They have been trying to do that again and they are going to continue to do that—Kuwait and Bahrain and Saudi. So with extra money it is exactly what they would try to do. They are focused on eastern Saudi Arabia. They are focused on Kuwait. They are focused again—I mean, they have stated very unequivocally that their goal in Bahrain is to empower Shi'ites and to overthrow the monarchy there. So those goals become much more attainable with money and with extra units that are focusing on those.

Chairman ROYCE. What surprises me is the sheer amount of weaponry. You know, as I mentioned, when I was in Haifa, I mean, at that point in time it was tens of thousands of rockets that they had at their disposal and now it is maybe five fold that.

So that is over a decade now. Let us just look at Hamas. It is giving its funding, its weapons, its training from Iran. We go to March 2011. Israel intercepted the Victoria—intercepted that ship off its coast.

There were C–704 cruise missiles—as well as a lot of mortars, but cruise missiles capable of targeting Israeli shipping and ports—that Israel said were bound for Hamas in Gaza.

Then you have got on March 5th they intercepted a ship in the Red Sea that Israel said was carrying Iranian advanced weaponry bound for militants in Gaza, possibly via Sudan. You see these M–302 long-range rockets now are what they are putting their money into.

Why in the middle of these negotiations would they run the risk of ramping up with resupply of even longer-range rockets? And this is another question I have.

I listened to this speech that the Ayatollah gave recently in which he said it was the duty, as I recall—the duty of every military man to mass produce ICBMs. Why would he, in the middle of negotiations, go out and transmit that kind of message through his armed services?

Mr. MODELL. The fundamental difference between the revolutionary agenda he has and the way that we would like them to come into the mainstream international community. It is as simple as that.

He separates the nuclear negotiations. Like you said, the only reason he has come forth for the nuclear negotiations is out of dire economic necessity. That has nothing to do with his revolutionary agenda, which they are continuing to push day in day out.

And that is what they—and that is the message, quite frankly, that he plays to his domestic audience and he wanted us to know as well. They are looking for—he said it and Foreign Minister Zarif has repeatedly said, we are not looking for rapprochement with the West.

We hope that these will lead to common ground and nothing more than that. We are going to continue to push forth in our support to militants in Gaza. We are going to continue to push forth all of our objectives in the region, which I have stated over and over in this paper and you guys have said as well.

And when you look at the bases of operation that they have that are expanding in places like Sudan and Ethiopia and others, all of that doesn't with a nuclear agreement.

Chairman ROYCE. I am out of time. We will go to Mr. Engel.

Mr. ENGEL. Thank you, Mr. Chairman. Let me start with you, Dr. Sachs. How is Israel likely to view a comprehensive Iranian nuclear deal?

Will they see it as one that empowers Iran and allows Iran a freer hand on destabilizing activities in the region?

Mr. SACHS. Thank you, Mr. Engel.

The question is in part who in Israel. The government and almost everyone would view it with great suspicion. There is very little trust in Iran, in the intentions of the Islamic Republic.

There is some hope among some that a deal, if it were stringent enough, might help delay somewhat the advancement of the nuclear program, and so in that sense there may be some minor relief.

But Israel, as I mentioned, will be very concerned that any deal will bring about rapprochement between the U.S. and Iran would bring about a relief of all the sanctions and would most importantly make others in the international community go to sleep on this issue.

Israel would very much like everyone—itself, the United States and everyone else—to remember that this problem will remain. I imagine that the reaction in Israel probably will have to a deal along the lines that we have been hearing will be negative.

But the question is on the nuance of a negative. Israel may view it as a terrible deal that it cannot live with. If the terms are strict enough, it may view it as a step that perhaps will halt something that it views as very bad, maybe one that it can live with in the meantime.

Mr. ENGEL. In your testimony, you alluded to Israel commonality with some of the Sunni Arab states such as—you didn't say it but such as Saudi Arabia or United Arab Emirates on Iran—similar outlooks.

Could you talk a little bit about that?

Mr. SACHS. Certainly. There is, as others have noted, there is a very common concern with Iran. I do think, though, the reasons are quite different. The Arab neighbors of Iran have longstanding challenges with the Islamic Republic and even with Iran itself.

There is geopolitical issues and there is, of course, the Sunni-Shi'a divide that has really engulfed the Middle East at the moment. All these things are things that Israel is not concerned about.

Israel is first and foremost concerned about the two main issues we've been talking about today—the nuclear program and Iran's very active destabilizing activity in the rest of the region. And so there is room for cooperation which is very important, is room on the nuclear issue, is room on closing Iran's opportunity for activity abroad. But it stems from a different cause. I will add one more thing, which is that the public aspect of this alliance is very difficult.

The ''Arab street,'' or public opinion, is very sensitive to the Palestinian issue and especially these days and this makes it harder for Israel and Saudi Arabia to publicly engage, although there have been—even despite that there have been public instances of meetings, for example, of former chiefs of intelligence between the two countries.

In other words, there is hope on this, although there, I think, are some limitations.

Mr. ENGEL. Thank you. Let me talk a little bit about Iranian support for Hamas and perhaps, Dr. Takeyh, I can start with you. There have been some differences between Hamas and Iran since they take different sides in Syria.

Iran supports Assad while Hamas opposes him. How do you see this playing out? People have said that Hamas is more internationally isolated now than it has been in the past—isolated from Egypt, isolated perhaps from Syria. Is there a chance that this might reduce Iran—that it would cause Iran to reduce its material and moral support for Hamas?

Mr. TAKEYH. I think historically the Palestinian rejectionist group that has had more in common with Iran has been the Palestinian Jihad. However, Iran has always had an instrumentalized approach to Hamas, namely, whenever Hamas has an agenda that is common with Iran, which is essentially intrusion against Israel, then they come together.

The notion of supporting Palestinian rejectionist groups writ large has been the central aspect of Iran policy so I don't necessarily think that there is going to be any adjustment in that, particularly at a time when this has some degree of street popularity.

Mr. ENGEL. Is it surprising to you—I know Iran has been supporting and supplying Hamas for many years but in doing so it is— Iran by doing so is crossing the Shi'a-Sunni divide in order to help the Palestinians. Is that something that we should be alarmed about?

Mr. TAKEYH. Iran has always suggested that its policy in the region is not a sectarian one—that it will essentially make common cause with Sunnis that share its agenda. It is the Sunni street that likes to portray Iran mostly as a Shi'ite state but essentially Iran has always tried to have a pan-Islamic approach and to essentially unite Shi'ites and Sunnis that share the same common objectives.

Now, that has become very difficult as the region has become subject to such sectarian division and Iran at this particular point is more closely aligned with Shi'a state but is always open to dealing with radical Sunni groups that share its perspective.

Mr. ENGEL. Mr. Modell, do you have a comment on that?

Mr. MODELL. The only thing I would say is when you look at the—when you look at the trajectory of transnational organized crime and Iran's collaboration with, like, a group like Lebanese Hezbollah, for instance, there are a considerable amount of Sunnis and Shi'a that are involved in those activities, you know, I don't think Iran has any problem crossing, for political convenience, any——

Mr. ENGEL. Thank you. Thank you, Mr. Chairman.

Chairman ROYCE. Mr. Chris Smith of New Jersey. Oh, he is going to defer to Ileana Ros-Lehtinen of Florida.

Ms. ROS-LEHTINEN. He is a gentleman. Thank you so much, Mr. Chairman, as you are.

Iran agreeing to the weak and easy to live up to interim agreement is just another ploy by the regime to win concessions and buy more time, and now that the deadline is quickly approaching an extension must not be given.

Instead, we need to start reexamining our sanctions program against Iran and ways to counter its illicit and destabilizing activities. We have no reason to trust this regime but we have decades of proof that shows Iran's true colors.

One of the very first acts of terror of this current regime in Iran was responsible for, after the '79 Islamic revolution, the seizure of the U.S. Embassy in Tehran. Led by a group of students but spiritual followers of Khomeini, these terrorists held 52 American diplomats and citizens hostage for nearly 450 days.

Iran has been a United States-designated state sponsor of terrorism since '84. It has been repeatedly redesignated by the State Department as a country of particular concern for its continued and flagrant abuse of religious minorities and the regime has been highlighted year after year by our State Department's country reports on human rights practices for its abysmal human rights record.

Then, of course, we turn to the nuclear issue. Iran was discovered to have been operating a covert nuclear program for decades in an attempt to create a nuclear weapon, a program that we did not find for years.

So what confidence do we have that Iran—that we will be able to catch Iran cheating again? That is a question. Now, there are six U.N. Security Council resolutions against Iran's nuclear programs, resolutions that demand that Iran not be allowed to enrich any uranium at all, and yet Iran continues to be in violation of those resolutions.

It continues to make progress on its nuclear and ballistic missile programs. Yet, from the very beginning administration after administration have failed to hold the Iranian regime accountable for all of these aggressions—for all of these aggressive acts.

The hostages of the '79 crisis have yet to receive their justice. Our policy must be to seek justice for our citizens who have been victims of terrorism, hold the terrorists such as Iran accountable, and appropriately compensate the victims.

The administration, this one as have many others before it with other rogue regimes, believes that a nuclear agreement can open up avenues for further cooperation.

But we saw this with North Korea and others that this is never the case. What is the danger in dealing with Iran as if its nuclear program exists in a vacuum? This is somehow that it is somehow not related to all of Iran's other illicit and problematic areas.

In the administration's continued negotiations with Iran, we have managed to alienate and even anger some of our traditional partners and allies in the region and our credibility just keeps going lower.

At what cost will this nuclear deal impact our foreign policy and objectives in the Middle East in its totality, whether an agreement is reached or not?

And what would be the benefit of alienating all of these countries like Saudi Arabia, like the UAE and even Israel, who has a very real and existential concern over Iran's nuclear program, in favor of an Iranian nuclear agreement that many believe will not go far enough?

What would be the benefit of alienating all of our allies? Thank you, Doc.

Mr. TAKEYH. Thanks. I will begin this. I think there has always been something unusual and peculiar about an arms control approach because it essentially assumes that you can segregate your arms control technical disputes with all the other range of disputes.

So in order to have an arms control approach you have to continuously use the phrase yes, but. Yes, the Supreme Leader is an anti-Semite who denies the Holocaust but nevertheless he can be a suitable custodian of sensitive nuclear technology.

Yes, Iran is a revisionist state that tends to disrespect international norms but it can nevertheless be a suitable adherent to various protocols in terms of—in terms of proliferation.

So you have to continuously use the phrase yes, but it doesn't matter, and thus has always been very unusual around arms control pressure. The joint plan of action that you mentioned has one particularly problematic provision to it, namely, that it suggests the final agreement that is negotiated will have a sunset clause.

It will have an expiration date. Ali Khamenei recently mentioned that he wants to build up to 190,000 centrifuges after an expiration of the sunset clause, which Iranians wanted to be 5 to 7 years. He can build 190,000 centrifuges with impunity.

He can build a heavy water reactor with impunity. He can build 1.5 million centrifuges with impunity and he can upgrade those to a level of high advancement and high velocity centrifuges.

Ms. ROS-LEHTINEN. Thank you.

Mr. TAKEYH. In essence, Iran can become a nuclear weapon state with alacrity.

Ms. ROS-LEHTINEN. Yes, but—thank you very much. Thank you, Mr. Chairman.

Chairman ROYCE. We go now to Mr. Gerry Connolly of Virginia.

Mr. CONNOLLY. Thank you, Mr. Chairman, and thank you for having this hearing. Thank you to our witnesses.

Picking up on your last statement there, Dr. Takeyh, would it be better if the United States simply disengaged and announced we are no longer talking to Iran about its nuclear development program?

Mr. TAKEYH. No, I don't think that is true at all. I think this process of negotiations has been helpful. I think an alternative to the deficient arms control agreement——

Mr. CONNOLLY. Could I interrupt you?

Mr. TAKEYH [continuing]. Is a better arms control agreement.

Mr. CONNOLLY. Okay. Of course, and in a perfect world it is even better. But given the fact that our two nations haven't really even talked to each other for a long time, you know, trying to break the ice so that we kind of get a little bit comfortable with each other's styles and where we are coming from would kind of make sense in a negotiating posture, would it not?

Mr. TAKEYH. I don't have any objections to the process.

Mr. CONNOLLY. Do you think that the Phase 1 Interim Agreement suitably meets that need?

Mr. TAKEYH. I think the joint plan of action has some constructive dimensions to it and I think it has some aspects to it which were unwise, particularly the sunset clause.

Mr. CONNOLLY. Do we have—you know, Ronald Reagan popularized the Russian phrase ''doveryai no proveryai''—trust but verify. How would you assess that level of trust between the two countries and what are the mechanisms we need to have—to be able to have sufficient trust to go forward?

Mr. TAKEYH. Well, I would suggest in terms of arms control we should negotiate an agreement whose restrictions are permanent and not subject to an expiration clause and that way the program can remain limited and therefore subject to intrusive verification that can monitor compliance.

Upon expiration of the sunset clause, Iran will have an industrial-sized nuclear program and persistent diversion of nuclear resources from an industrial-sized nuclear program are difficult to defect irrespective of inspection modality.

Mr. CONNOLLY. Do you see any kind of cleavage between the Rouhani government and the Supreme Leader on the subject and how might that affect, you know, the negotiations for a permanent agreement?

Mr. TAKEYH. I have only access to the public commentary, public speeches and what they say to their audiences and in that particular sense, Congressman, I don't know if there are too many cleavages between the Supreme Leader and this President on the nuclear issue.

Their style of representation is different but on the nuclear issue I have not detected the cleavages that are suggested.

Mr. CONNOLLY. Is there reason to believe that there is an awareness in Tehran in governing circles that this really is a pretty important issue existentially for Iran, that whatever your desire for the symbolism and the prestige and all that, this is potentially a direct threat to Iran and its future and the stakes are so high that you actually have to get serious. I mean, you are going to have to weigh just how important nuclear development is to you—that is to say the development of fissile material for a bomb versus your very future. How would you assess that awareness in Tehran? Because I think that is also key to the posture in a negotiating settlement and how we respond to perceived sincerity or lack thereof.

Mr. TAKEYH. I think during his tenure as Supreme Leader, which began in 1989 which makes Ali Khamenei one of the longest serving leaders in the Middle East, the tragedy of Ali Khamenei, which has become Iran's tragedy, is that he has persistently subordinated national interest to ideological compulsions and at this particular point I think there are some in the system that recognize the necessity of having a nuclear program but also the importance of reviving the economy.

That particular balance doesn't seem entirely obvious in the way he talks about the nuclear issue. What he says in his private councils I have no access to. I only know what he says to his audiences.

Mr. CONNOLLY. Yes. And do you think—some people see Rouhani genuinely having evolved and creating some political space, frankly, between the government and the Supreme Leader on this and some other issues. I would say it is just illusory. Rouhani comes right out of the leadership circles.

Mr. TAKEYH. Well, he has certainly been part of the leadership for a long time and he has been part of the nuclear program for a long time. As early as the 1980s he was one of the officials responsible for procuring nuclear material.

So he has been involved in it for a long time and he has committed himself to nuclear advancement for a long time. I think the way he looks at the nuclear program is trying to situate it in the larger context of Iranian needs. However, that doesn't seem to be the case with those who he has to interlocutor with.

Mr. CONNOLLY. Dr. Sachs, in the brief time I have left did you want to comment? And then I am done.

Mr. SACHS. Thank you, sir. Yes, I just—I think we should point out that the very real dangers of the Iranian nuclear program, ones that Israelis and others are extremely concerned about, are true with a deal to a certain degree. They are certainly true without a deal.

And so the questions of a deal are very important on exactly how they are phrased, what kind of modalities there are for inspections and others. But the lack of a deal, I would just caution, does not solve our problem by any means.

Mr. CONNOLLY. Thank you very much, and Mr. Modell, I didn't mean to discriminate against you. I have just run out of time.

Mr. MODELL. Okay.

Mr. CONNOLLY. Thank you, Mr. Chairman.

Chairman ROYCE. We go to—certainly. Mr. Chris Smith of New Jersey.

Mr. SMITH. Thank you, Mr. Chairman. Thank you for calling this very important hearing. Dr. Takeyh, let me ask you, on page 2 of your testimony you mentioned—and this is your quote:

> "In Khamenei's depiction, America is a crestfallen imperial state hastily retreating from the region. Whatever compunctions Tehran may have had about American power greatly diminished with the spectacle over Syria where Washington's redlines were erased with the same carelessness that they were initially drawn."

Could you elaborate on it? I think that is a very strong statement and how much of that do you think might be true? But impression or perception sometimes is as important, particularly in the eyes of a mischievous actor like Iran.

Secondly, I would like to ask you, you did point out on page 6 that human rights would have to assume a high place in our negotiations. Iran must be pressed to honor international norms on treatment of its citizens.

I have raised with Secretary Kerry on several occasions and other representatives from the administration my disappointment that human rights were not at least in part integrated in the negotiations on the nuclear issue and in mid-June, just June 18th, I had a hearing on human rights in North Korea and former Special Envoy to Sudan Andrew Natsios who is also the co-chairman of the Committee for Human Rights in North Korea pointed out that in the Six-Party Talks we left it out there and when they collapsed in totality we had nothing when it came to human rights.

And, you know, we have raised Saeed Abedini, Amir Hekmati and Robert Levinson time and time again and said make that a part. Your thoughts on that and any other who would like to speak today.

Mr. TAKEYH. On the first point, I think the Supreme Leader has given two speeches, most recently July 7th that the chairman mentioned where he called for 190,000 centrifuges, potentially, where he has discounted the possibility of an American military strike explicitly and directly.

So he no longer fears the notion that the United States has all its options on the table. At least that is what he tells his audiences and he seems very comfortable with the notion that his state is no longer going to be subject to American nuclear military retribution.

Israelis I can't speak to because he hasn't spoken to it. As far as human rights, as you recall, Congressman, my colleague, Mark Lagon, and I have come and seen you and seen Congressman Deutch about establishing a human rights commission to essentially bring greater legislative focus on this issue.

In previous arms control negotiations with the Soviet Union the issue of human rights was brought up. That doesn't necessarily mean that agreement was contingent or linked to that but nevertheless it was brought up by George Shultz and others in negotiating with the Soviet Union.

Similarly, I think, could be happening. Human rights concerns tend to come from the legislative branch. The executive branch tends to be very hesitant about incorporating human rights in its diplomacy.

The Human Rights Bureau in the State Department was essentially conceived during Henry Kissinger's time and there is nobody less concerned about human rights than Henry Kissinger, and it was essentially because of legislative pressure.

So if there is going to be human rights discussions in nuclear diplomacy and international diplomacy that initiative has to come from the Hill.

Mr. MODELL. Congressman, if I could just say a word on that. When Rouhani was elected, one of the things that he said—and this was, of course, in collaboration with the Supreme Leader—was he had sort of a three-phased approach. One was the immediate urgency—contending with the immediate urgency of repairing the economy.

I mean, that first and foremost was on the top of agenda of everybody. Once he did that it was about shoring up all the support, shoring up the power of the regime itself, and then if they got around to it, it was about going and starting to answer some of the questions about human rights.

Now, of course, we have seen a three- or four-fold increase in human rights related abuses since Rouhani has taken office.

The other point I would make too, you know, when you look at the type of international inspection and verification and monitoring regime that you are going to have to create in the aftermath of an agreement, I think people need to keep in mind something that it has taken the Iranians maybe 10 or 15 years—particularly, the last 10 or 15 years—to build up an extremely intricate global apparatus for evading sanctions and, you know, the idea that we can sign an agreement, think that we are going to be able to figure out all the military dimensions, all—figure out every way in which they are proliferating, I think is naive and we better start thinking very soon about how we are going to—how we are going to actually come up with a new containment strategy for doing things like that.

And when we talk about the GCC partners and our allies, you know, I think those are enduring bilateral security partnerships. I don't think that there is any jointness to be—you know, to be really taken seriously on the part of the GCC countries.

But they are shaken by the fact that they are going to be facing a nuclear Iran. The global multilateral containment strategy that we need to come up with is critical at this point in time.

Mr. SMITH. Thank you. I see I am out of time.

Chairman ROYCE. Without objection. We will go to Mr. David Cicilline.

Mr. CICILLINE. Thank you, Mr. Chairman, and thank you to the witnesses for your very important testimony. I want to just begin, Dr. Takeyh, with the statement that you made about, you know, a better arms control agreement is preferred over a deficient one, which I think everyone agrees with.

But to focus for a moment on this sunset clause, is it your assessment that the Iranians think at the conclusion of that sunset clause that they are likely to be—or before the conclusion of the sunset clause there is likely to be an engagement with the United States and the other partners about an extension to that agreement or is it your assessment they think once it is over all bets are off and they can robustly proceed with their nuclear weapons program?

Mr. TAKEYH. The notion that once the sunset clause has expired and Iran is treated as any other member of the NPT and therefore can expand its nuclear resources and installations according to its own determination is something that the Supreme Leader has said. It is something that Iran's chief negotiator Abbas Araghchi has said as well.

Mr. CICILLINE. Does anyone have a different view of that? Okay. I would like to next turn to the destabilizing impact of Iran in Iraq and I apologize if you spoke to this a little bit earlier.

But I would like any of the witnesses' comment what you think Iran's goals are in Iraq today and whether or not the Iranian interests are aligned tightly with the Maliki government and what is the likely impact of Iran's ongoing engagement in Iraq over the long term.

Mr. MODELL. Congressman, to answer the question, everything that I have seen is that Iran is desperately trying to keep Maliki in place. They have benefited tremendously by having him in place over the last decade. They don't want him to go away and if they do—because if he does go away what comes next. They are not really sure.

I think that there are certain Iranians—pragmatic-minded Iranians who look at the way Maliki has failed, you know, miserably in leading Iraq over the last 10 years and asking themselves why Maliki didn't do a better job of, you know, governing over Sunnis and Kurds.

But they are desperately trying to keep him there. They are desperately trying to keep the Kurds from breaking away but I think their long-term interest is stability and its continuing to build the base of support that they have.

But the problem with the base of support that they are building is that it is mainly comprised of Shi'a militia forces and those Shi'a militia forces, as we know, are not loyal to the government in any way whatsoever.

So if you are ever going to hope for some long-term healing of the sectarian divide in that country in the brutal fighting that is going on, that is not the way to do it. So they are not really part of the long-term solution, to be honest.

Mr. CICILLINE. Dr. Sachs.

Mr. SACHS. I think this touches on a very severe problem that Iran has that Ray raised earlier. Iran as the major Shi'a power would very much like to present itself not as a Shi'a power simply because the vast majority of Muslims around the world are Sunni.

And so it would much prefer to present itself as a leading power in this part of the world rather than a Shi'a one. The animosity toward Israel is part of that. The best way to curry favor with people who disagree with you on the Shi'a-Sunni divide is to adopt the same enemy that many Muslims unfortunately perceive in Israel.

In Iraq and Syria and Lebanon and elsewhere, Iran is finding itself, however, on the side of what is becoming more and more a sectarian divide, something which the adversaries of Iran—not Israel but Saudi Arabia and others—are seeing very much as a sectarian divide.

I think this is the common theme now of the Middle East and really overshadows most of what we are seeing across the region. It is not necessarily in Iran's interest but it is very worrisome. I agree with Scott very much, it is very worrisome. It is becoming more and more, partly through Iran's actions, a sectarian divide.

Mr. CICILLINE. And Dr. Sachs, you mentioned in your testimony that if Iran develops a nuclear weapon that you believe that the transfer outside of the state or outside of Iran is a long shot.

Would you explain kind of what you think argues—from Iran's perspective why they are likely to do that or not do that because obviously they are developing a nuclear weapon and then the transfer to an actor outside of Iran is a further complication.

Mr. SACHS. I was quoting the views—the common views in Israel, not necessarily my own. But I do think that by and large it is a long shot. Of course, it is a long shot with huge ramifications.

So even if the risk of its happening is low, the damage of it happening would be enormous. The main concern with Iran is whether it itself would use nuclear weapons and on that many Israelis and others believe that since it believes Israel has second strike capabilities, and although its goals seem unreasonable, its manner of pursuing them has been rational, and as a rational actor, therefore, you would expect it not to use these nuclear weapons in mutually assured destruction.

It is a very grim reality, one which I very much hope we do not get to, but it may be stable. The transfer to other parties is tied to this as well.

The question is whether they could believe that they could do this without detection, whether they would believe that Israel would not think that it is them, whether this kind of transfer would get them out of the grim mutually assured destruction logic.

It is certainly possible that they would try to do it. I think it is unlikely because the chances of avoiding this kind of mutually assured destruction logic from the Israeli side is low.

Mr. CICILLINE. Thank you. Thank you, Mr. Chairman. I yield back.

Chairman ROYCE. Thank you. We go now to Mr. Dana Rohrabacher of California.

Mr. ROHRABACHER. Thank you very much, Mr. Chairman. This is to the panel—how popular are the mullahs in their own country? Are we talking about 10 percent of the people support them? Twenty percent? Fifty percent?

What is the real level of support that mullahs have in their own country?

Mr. TAKEYH. I think that is very difficult to estimate. However, I would suggest in the aftermath of the 2009 election—the fraudulent election of 2009—that was really a watershed moment when the regime essentially forfeited a considerable amount of its popular legitimacy.

The Islamic Republic became more Islamic and less republic. So whatever the popularity it had which, as you mentioned, was always very marginal, has, in my opinion, diminished considerably after that particular election.

Mr. ROHRABACHER. Could I prod you a little bit more? How about giving me just a guesstimate?

Mr. TAKEYH. Possibly 10 percent of the population. But it is the 10 percent of the population that it can mobilize and bring to the street and essentially dominate.

Mr. ROHRABACHER. All right. And tacit support another 10 percent or 20 percent?

Mr. TAKEYH. It is very difficult to judge that. I think at this particular point the regime is quite unpopular because of its performance, because of its ideology and because of the infamy that has come because of misconduct.

I certainly don't think it can survive a plebiscite or a fair election.

Mr. ROHRABACHER. Okay. What about our next——

Mr. MODELL. Congressman, I think that you ask one of the most difficult questions. We have spent years in the government trying to figure out exactly the answer to that question and part of the problem with polling in that country is people are afraid to speak their minds, particularly when it is not very delicately done.

So to be honest with you, I don't—I don't know but I can tell you, though, a reflection of the fact that you don't—I mean, you may have a significant amount of people there who are unhappy and don't support the mullahs and the regime but that hasn't translated into a military movement inside that is willing to do what the Green Movement did in 2009.

Mr. SACHS. I am no expert on Iranian internal affairs but I would at least point out that Iran has a very smart way of going about ruling a country not through democracy, which is to have something that looks sometimes like democracy.

These hybrid regimes where there are meaningful elections that have some kind of meaning but are not truly free—the candidates, of course, are vetted ahead of time—this actually allows for a lot of steam, a lot of vent to go out. It allows people to change some of the policies without undermining the fundamental regime.

So even if the hard core support is very low, we could still find a system that is stable both because of some fear and oppression but also because there is a smart design to it, much smarter than extreme totalitarian dictatorship.

Mr. ROHRABACHER. So let me note for the record, Mr. Chairman, that none of our witnesses were willing to actually put a number down in terms of what they think the level of support for the mullahs.

Now, we depend on you guys. You know, this is—you are supposed to be telling us these things. I would suggest that the mullahs are very unpopular with about 90 percent of the people but I don't know that—I was hoping you were going to give me some guidance on that.

But we do know that among the people of Iran there are not just Persians. What percentage of the population is Persian?

Mr. MODELL. I think it is—the last time I looked I think it was 68—67 to 68 percent.

Mr. ROHRABACHER. So you have about 40 percent or so—30 to 40 percent——

Mr. MODELL. Thirty to forty percent that are Azeris and I know there is Kurds and others.

Mr. ROHRABACHER. Kurds, Baloch—people such as that. Is there—and the popularity among the mullahs among the minorities I imagine would be even less than among the young Persians. Is there any reason why—I mean, frankly, when we talk about Iran I hear all kinds of analysis of the power flow and the dynamics of the Iranian regime itself.

I rarely hear any specific suggestions of how we get rid of it and I would suggest, as I have in the past, that we need to be looking at the opposition. If it is only at 10 percent, which we don't know—we are not even willing to speculate that support level—there should be lots of people there including those people who are non-Persian who we might be able to mobilize against the regime. But I don't think we have been doing that, have we?

Mr. MODELL. No, we have not. Not at all, to be honest with you. I would like to make one comment on 2009. So when 2009 came and the aftermath of the Presidential elections, as you recall, and the Green Movement started and as it grew the Supreme Leader and the regime completely underestimated it. And once they did realize the dimension of the problem, the Supreme Leader said okay, now we have to come together.

And when we are talking about a whole of government solution, something that is exactly what they did and it cleared out Evin Prison and they got everybody together and there is all sort of interagency differences over there disappeared as they very effectively dismantled that movement.

But the key thing is this: It was in 2009 as it started to gain momentum that some of the leaders of that movement, and this is publicly known, were reaching out to the United States and saying what do we do—where do we go—can you give us any guidance? And they weren't necessarily looking to overthrow the regime.

That was never their stated goal. But it was a crack in the—it was a potential real crack in the foundation that we could have assisted and we did not do that.

Mr. ROHRABACHER. We have been waiting for other people to make those cracks. We should start helping making them ourselves. Thank you very much, Mr. Chairman.

Chairman ROYCE. Thank you, Mr. Rohrabacher. We go now to Brad Schneider of Illinois.

Mr. SCHNEIDER. Thank you, Mr. Chairman, and thank you to the panel for sharing your insights and thoughts. Dr. Takeyh, let me start with you and I think it was you who said, you know, one of the real concerns about any type of negotiation to an agreement with Iran is trying to achieve a durable agreement with an unreliable partner and like you I share the concern of discussion of a determined—in particular, the idea of a discussion of a determined number of years. I think it should be at the very least generations if we can't get the permanent agreement.

But more broadly, do you think it is possible for a deal with Iran no matter how well structured it is on the document to be effectively enforced?

Mr. TAKEYH. I think you have to kind of think about the importance of nuclear capability within Iran's larger regional policy. At a time when it has an aggressive regional policy it makes sense to have nuclear capability.

In the Gulf today, there is an imbalance of conventional power. The Saudis and others have greater conventional strength simply because they have access to the American military supplies and Iran does not have an access to international military supplies and doesn't have an indigenous arms industry.

So the way Iranians have tried to affect that imbalance of power is by developing unconventional capabilities—missiles and unconventional weapons, chemical weapons. And so nuclear weapons fit into that particular equation and so long as Iran has hegemonic aspiration it will make sense for it to have nuclear capability.

As Hassan Rouhani said in his memoirs—he has published four—he is very self-reflective—the last one he said look, there is a—he always talks about it as a peaceful nuclear weapon but he said the problem with our peaceful nuclear weapon is it got caught before it reached its objectives.

So since then, they have to balance nuclear sophistication and enlargement with economic contraction and that has been the struggle. During the Ahmadinejad era, of course, they put privilege on nuclear enlargement.

Iran, as a matter of revolutionary ideology—the Islamic Republic as a matter of revolutionary ideology tends to suspect international norms as unfair and international organizations as conspiring against it.

That includes the IAEA and the U.N. Security Council, whose resolutions it has rejected as politically contrived. So it makes it less reliable of an arms control partner than the example that is often cited, mainly the Soviet Union.

Mr. SCHNEIDER. Let me turn to Dr. Sachs, because in the context of Iran looking to bolster its capacity—hegemonic capacity with unconventional you talked about the full spectrum of Iranian activity. Does the support of Hezbollah—Palestinian Islamic jihad fit within the context of that trying to extend their reach?

Mr. SACHS. Well, the problem, of course, with negotiations around that is what can you do within the context of negotiations. So the problem, I think, for many Israelis is, indeed, as we have mentioned before—that these negotiations don't include all these different aspects—the full spectrum, as you say.

The problem is, of course, whether or not you can get a deal in all of that. The question is the capability, even through sanctions, which were very stringent, can those sanctions bring about Iranian capitulation on everything or is there a chance of bringing it about the nuclear issue.

I don't know that we can on the nuclear issue and it certainly looks like we are not going to have it by July 20th, although never say never. But the chances of having it on the full spectrum are even lower.

And so the very difficult dilemma, I think, from a policy perspective is does one opt for trying to go for something which one cannot achieve or does one focus very concretely on the specific issues that maybe one can. The spectrum remains, though, and this is, I think, a very important point.

Even if there is a deal on the nuclear issue not only will the nuclear issue still be relevant and important the day after—in fact, it will be more important to keep a watchful eye—the other issues that we have been raising here today will be perhaps even more important with Iran freed from sanctions, or most of the sanctions at least, and free to do many other things that it can't do at the moment.

Mr. SCHNEIDER. I agree with you and I know last month this committee passed unanimously the Hezbollah sanctions bill that would limit or prohibit their access to international banking and thwart some of that relationship. I am hopeful that that full House and then the Senate will pass that this month.

Dr. Modell, as you look at what is happening in the region and the threat of holding Iran to account on the full spectrum on their nuclear program, and you talked about the inherent need that we have to understand their potential military dimension—their weaponization, their delivery systems—an agreement that just focusses on enrichment how do you see that—what risks do you see that that leaves open, going forward?

Mr. MODELL. Well, I think the difference—for me, I see risks no matter what kind of a deal we strike, to be honest with you, because I think that the time—I think somebody has mentioned it here—one of the panel has mentioned it here that time is key.

Three, five, seven years—it doesn't matter because when that time expires the revolutionary—you know, the conventional agenda is not going to stop and if you truly believe that they are after nuclear weapons why can't they suspend that?

They have a long-term vision here—why can't they suspend that for 3 to 5 years and pick up where they left off? Another thing I would mention too in the context of these negotiations it shouldn't be surprising that they are putting limitations—the Iranians, that is—on the breadth of these negotiations.

They have got their—they very clearly spelled out their own red lines. They won't even talk about ballistic missiles, you know, in these—in the context of these negotiations.

Neither will they talk about rapprochement with the West or even human rights. So I think regardless of the——I mean, I am hoping for a good——the best deal possible but I think you need at least 10 to 15 years to build up the trust that is going to be required and the ability. And it is not just the trust.

It is not just, you know, good behavior over time. It is for us to build up the mechanisms we need globally to figure out if they are cheating and we can't rely solely on the IAEA to do that.

Mr. SCHNEIDER. Thank you. I am out of time. I will just say that against a regime that thinks in millennium and carries forward a long-term vision, talking about years or decades just doesn't seem sufficient. And with that, I will yield back.

Chairman ROYCE. We go to Mr. Steve Chabot of Ohio.

Mr. CHABOT. Thank you, Mr. Chairman. I thank you for holding this important hearing this morning. As the recent crisis in Iraq began to unfold, the administration initially welcomed Iranian engagement in an effort to quickly resolve the issue, although many experts cautioned against such policies and I would put myself in that latter category.

I think it is——we have to be very wary of any involvement with Iran. But I would be interested to hear the panel's take on what is——what is Iran's strategy with respect to Iraq?

What are they trying to accomplish? What should we be particularly wary of? What dangers are they——either the short or long term in rubbing elbows with Iran here? Maybe thinking we are getting something now that we want but long term we have made a deal with the devil here. Mr. Takeyh.

Mr. TAKEYH. I think the objectives of the Iranian Government at this point and have been since 2003 to consolidate the power of the Shi'i majority.

They are essentially aware that some degree of Sunni participation could help and the civil war is not necessarily in their interest because it will have spillover effects.

In terms of the Maliki government, they probably have their dissatisfactions with the way Prime Minister Maliki has ruled but overall their approach is in the middle of a crisis you don't change horses.

That was the case in Assad as well in the sense that they didn't want Assad to be dislodged and replaced with another member of the Alawite family. So you go war with the army you have, in essence. And long term essentially to remove Iraq from the Councils of Sunni Arab States, have a weakened Iraq——Shi'i dominated Iraq——that to some extent relies on Iran for its objectives and commerce.

Mr. CHABOT. Thank you. Would any of the other members like to touch——Mr. Modell.

Mr. MODELL. The only thing I would——the only thing I would add to that is I think there——we shouldn't underestimate how many Iraqis are against the idea of Iran's influence in that country growing.

So when we are reading reports here that may sound like we are sort of dovetailing, you know, in terms of dealing with ISIS, Iranians are working against that cause. We want to work against that cause.

But a lot of Iraqis are very wary about the growth of Iran's role in that country. So I would be cautious about saying that it is— it certainly is—I think it is more divisive over time than anything else.

Mr. CHABOT. Thank you. Dr. Sachs, anything you would like to add? Okay. Thank you.

At the recent talks over Iran's nuclear program in Vienna, Secretary Kerry mentioned that the international community needs tangible reassurance that Iran will not move to quickly develop nuclear weapons.

How can the administration develop an agreement to realistically prevent the Iranians from pursuing the weapons program, which I think, quite frankly, whatever we do they are bound and determined to accomplish this. But I know the administration continues to believe that there is some hope there.

How do you think a long-term nuclear agreement would affect Iran's interactions with terrorist groups in the region, for example, and what impact would a long-term nuclear agreement have on Iran's ability to influence its neighbors in the region? And whoever would like to take it is welcome to.

Mr. MODELL. I would say that they are—I tend to agree with you. I think regardless of the type of agreement we see, they have got an agenda to cross that threshold and weaponize and I think that we are going to, you know, in terms of figuring out what is it we need to do to figure out how to build a global apparatus to give ourselves the best chance of determining if they are cheating or not or if they are going to break out.

Quite frankly, I think we have had the last decade of realizing— enough time to realize that it is really hard to do these things.

There is enough evidence—the U.S. Government has collected enough evidence—and its allies—over the years of proliferation networks but they haven't been criminalized—adequately criminalized.

I think that there is a law enforcement aspect to this and it is not only U.S. but I think there is a global law enforcement aspect to this that needs to be improved because if you can—if we enable ourselves to better pursue law enforcement investigations that are related to nuclear proliferation it goes hand in hand with figuring out if they are cheating or not. I think that has been a real deficiency.

Mr. CHABOT. Thank you. Let me—go ahead, Dr. Sachs.

Mr. SACHS. Well, I think on the central issues that might allow for a reasonable deal, I don't think a good deal is possible and I agree that there is little chance that it would guarantee no development of nuclear weapons.

But certainly the plutonium track, the weaponization aspects of it and, of course, enrichment, both in terms of stocks of uranium— the stocks that are already there, but also technology and technology that might advance.

All these issues are crucial and, of course, are being raised. Another issue that was raised here today and is more problematic is the issue of delivery systems of ballistic missiles accurate enough and capable of doing this, and that is really important and perhaps one that might be deficient.

And, of course, verification is the main issue—the degree to how stringent the verification will be of compliance to this agreement will be crucial. None of this guarantees at all that Iran won't pursue it anyway. I would just caution, again, that the lack of a deal certainly does not guarantee that either.

Mr. CHABOT. Thank you. My time has expired, Mr. Chairman.

Chairman ROYCE. Thank you. We go to Dr. Ami Bera from California.

Mr. BERA. Thank you, Mr. Chairman. I think, Dr. Takeyh, you touched on that, at present, Iran doesn't have the military capabilities with conventional arsenals compared to Saudi Arabia and others in the region.

So, you know, from my perspective I think how they have tried to level the playing field and that balance of power is through this—you know, through the terror networks and so forth.

And in essence, you can almost draw a line from Iran to Maliki now to Assad to Hezbollah to Hamas as kind of that destabilizing force and, you know, if you think about some of the proxies.

I also—you know, I would be curious on your thought there.

Mr. TAKEYH. I think that is right. In 2006 and 2007, the current head of the Revolutionary Guards, General Jafari, before that he was kind of a strategic planner and he came up with something called mosaic defense, namely, that increasingly the United States will not invade another Middle Eastern country so the question is how do you adjust your defense posture in order to advance your objectives given that?

And essentially he came out with the ideals of asymmetrical defense, reliance on missile technology, proxy forces, and it was at that time that the role of Hezbollah in particular changed in Iranian calculations.

Hezbollah was no longer a political party with a military apparatus that Iranians try to have a greater say in the Lebanese society, but they essentially became an auxiliary of the Iranian force and you see that manifestation particularly in Syria.

So that is essentially the way they think about their defense and unconventional weapons are essentially part of that.

Mr. BERA. In your words, Khamenei puts the ideologic interest ahead of the national interest and I think in your testimony is it accurate to say he sees the United States as a country in retreat from the region?

Mr. TAKEYH. That is right. That is what he says.

Mr. BERA. So if he is looking at things in that way and if we look at what has got us to this point, you know, clearly, the sanctions have been effective in bringing them to the table.

Clearly, the sanctions have been effective in creating some unrest and, you know, creating some real issues within the Iranian economy. Would now—doesn't appear to me now is the time for us to step back a little bit. Now is the time for us to actually continue to exert influence.

Mr. TAKEYH. I am not disagreeing with that. I think that is right. I would say that whatever leverage we have mobilized with sanctions and other measures have obviously been insufficient to discipline Iran into an agreement should there be an extension past July 20th.

As I was trying to suggest to Congressman Connolly, I don't oppose extension of the talks for another 6 months but I do think the administration has to respond to the question of what do you think is going to happen in the next 6 months that didn't happen in the previous ones. I think they should answer that question.

Mr. BERA. Because if we are negotiating with a regime that sees us in retreat, from my perspective I don't think that is the best position to negotiate from, I think.

Mr. TAKEYH. I would say at this point our coercive leverage has not been sufficient to compel an agreement.

Mr. BERA. Okay. So if—yes, I guess a lot of the others, if you would want to expand on that.

Mr. MODELL. I think I would tend to agree with you on this. The time for retreating on sanctions is wrong. I think that I have seen a number of Iranian leaders talking about it as a strategic opening and if after the biggest and the most effective sanctions regime we have ever put together isn't compelling them now after 6 months of negotiations with an economic knife at their throats to actually, you know, really be forthcoming about the most—the single most complex problem—in other words, the possible military dimensions of the program, then the answer is why are we letting up on sanctions now?

Mr. BERA. I would agree and that is not to be construed that we don't continue talking. But let us talk and negotiate from a place of strength.

Iran also has, you know, its own issues. You know, obviously the challenges that it is facing with the struggling al-Maliki government with the ISIL in Iraq and the Sunni uprising with Assad facing his own challenges.

So, you know, they certainly have to—in this negotiation they certainly have to fight a battle on multiple fronts as well and, you know, again, from a negotiating perspective I think my message to the administration and to—I do think we need to negotiate from a place of strength and that doesn't mean we don't—we stop talking.

It does mean we negotiate from strength. So thank you. I will yield back.

Mr. CHABOT. Thank you. The gentleman's time has expired. The gentleman from Illinois, Mr. Kinzinger, is recognized for 5 minutes.

Mr. KINZINGER. Well, thank you, Mr. Chairman, and thank you all for being here today and spending time with us. I just want to say off the bat the idea of—and I have heard administration officials talk, Secretary Kerry, and talking about what a potential final deal with Iran would look like, and in no way have they ruled out some level of enrichment.

You know, they will argue that well, we will keep it at a very low level of enrichment so breakout capability takes a long time and, you know, fine argument to make except the neighbors don't see it that way.

And what I think is also interesting is as we negotiate in one-two-three agreements around the world, there is a lot of areas we have denied our best allies the right to enrich. I think of South Korea, I think of the United Arab Emirates—these people that we say we are committed to a nuclear-free Korean Peninsula or Arab Peninsula and we don't give them that right.

And so to give the biggest enemy of the United States, I would argue, the right to do something that we deny to our best and closest allies will send a tragic message that America can't be trusted by its allies and it is not to be feared by its enemies and that is something that I fear.

I also am a veteran of Iraq and as a pilot there and I have noticed that it seems like every engagement, whether it is a war, whether it is some low-level engagement in the Middle East, that we have been involved in has somehow had the fingerprints of Iran all over it and I think of in Iraq it is estimated now that about half of the men and women that we lost in Iraq were a direct or indirect result of Iran itself. Whether it was their EFPs, the technology that they exported to the terrorists in Iraq, or whether it was even in some cases direct intervention. And we have seen that Iran continues to destabilize everywhere.

The other question I have, and I will ask you all to briefly answer this because I have some other questions, when we withdrew from Iraq—in 2003 we went in, we invaded, Iran seemed very eager to work with the United States at that point.

When we withdrew after 2011, what message did that send— pulled all the troops out of Iraq—what message did that send to Iran? If you could just very briefly answer.

Mr. TAKEYH. I think 2003 did come from, you know, an existential threat. We know that now and particularly with Rouhani's memoirs. Obviously, the general departure of the United States from the region and general hesitancy has emboldened Iran and I would actually go back to Syria before that and then Iraq became successor and affirmative to Syria.

Mr. KINZINGER. Okay.

Mr. MODELL. You know, Congressman, I just second that. I don't have anything to add other than in 2011 I think they viewed it as a strategic victory, to be honest with you, and they view U.S. withdrawal out of Afghanistan the same way.

Mr. SACHS. I think in general there is—the U.S. certainly has a problem in the Middle East of a perception of its weakness. It rightly or wrongly is perceived that way. Of course, the question is what kind of investment is the U.S. willing to do to avoid that, and it is a real one.

Mr. KINZINGER. I think—it is interesting to me. I have been studying a little bit recently a lot about the period between World War I and World War II where the world was war weary and they saw this rising threat in Europe and they did not confront it because of purveying war weariness.

Now, after World War I, I think the world had a right to be war weary. It lost millions of people, economies of scale destroyed. Today, I hear a lot of, frankly, my colleagues and talking heads talk about a war weariness in the United States of America.

And while I understand that some people certainly do experience war weariness, you know, there was no tax increase to fight the wars. Our economy was not changed based on the war in the Middle East, and while we lost too many people it really pales in comparison to what was lost at the end of World War II or in World War I and World War II.

At the end of World War II, Harry Truman came in and said—he didn't look at the American and say you are world weary—we have to leave Europe.

He looked at the American people and said, I know you are tired but the Soviet Union is going to be twice the size as it is today if we leave Europe and really motivated the American people.

My fear today is that we find ourselves in a situation where we are so eager to leave a period of conflict and warfare that we will do anything to get out and we hasten the day when a bigger war is going to happen, whether it is my generation or whether it is generations following me.

Lastly, I want to touch on as the situation in Iraq very tragically unfolds, I hear some people say that this is fine. You know, let the caliphate figure out that governing is not easy. They don't see governing like we do.

But they say that is great—let Iran get pulled into a quagmire in Iraq like we did, and I would argue that Iran defines quagmire quite differently than us.

We see losing 100 soldiers a month, as tragic as it is, as a quagmire and Iran does not. What are your all's thoughts on the idea of letting Iran get drug into a quagmire and how that would be?

Mr. TAKEYH. The same argument was made about Syria. Somehow, Iranians can manage in these convoluted situations with less cost and less casualties than we do simply because of their high reliance on proxies.

Mr. MODELL. I would just reiterate what I said before. I think that the longer time goes on with Iran being involved in Iraq, particularly militarily, the worse things get because they are going to rely on building up proxy forces there that are not necessarily loved by significant amounts of the population. So I think it is a negative force over time.

Mr. SACHS. Just briefly, I think we should also be very worried about what happens to these regions whether or not Iran gets caught in a quagmire. The ramifications for these countries—Syria, Iraq or others—is huge as well.

Mr. KINZINGER. Thank you, and I yield back.

Mr. CHABOT. The gentleman's time has expired. The gentleman from California, Mr. Sherman, who is the ranking member of the Terrorism, Nonproliferation, and Trade Subcommittee, is recognized for 5 minutes.

Mr. SHERMAN. Thank you, Mr. Chairman. I do want to just mention something for the record. I think it is absurd to think that the American people would be all gung ho for another war in the Middle East if only we had a President with a different personality.

No one thought that President Bush was a retiring violet but in the last year of his presidency I noticed no popular groundswell for an American invasion of Iran. I don't sense that today. I don't think it relates to whether—you know, what the personality of the President is.

I will say that under this administration we have paid a significant economic and diplomatic price for strengthening our sanctions on Iran, whereas in the Bush administration we didn't pass a single law of significance because the President prevented it and we didn't enforce any of the laws we had then.

So at least this President is willing to cause us to pay a diplomatic and economic price to control Iran, if not a price in the loss of American troops on the ground.

Dr. Sachs, you have got, obviously, the Shi'ite-Sunni split. Can Iran, al-Qaeda, and this new Islamic state aspire to be the leaders of extremist Islam? Can Iran aspire to that role or are they limited to the role of a protector of Shi'ites worldwide?

Mr. SACHS. They understand that they are very limited and they are especially limited in the context of this configuration, so if you look in previous years at the Shi'a-Sunni divide, it was not necessarily that salient.

The differences in identity were not necessarily expressed. Other issues, national and other, were much stronger.

But in the context of the Middle East today where the Sunni-Shi'a divide is so strong, it is hard to see Iran really taking leadership in the Arab world, and this is something that is quite different than in the past where they and Hezbollah, for example, held the mantle of fighting Israel.

Mr. SHERMAN. I see that Russia seems more positively disposed to Assad and Tehran. Is this because have a very small Shi'ite population in their own country and they are near abroad and so they don't see Iran as an ideological threat but they do see extremist Sunni groups as an ideological threat?

Mr. SACHS. I don't know, Sir. I doubt it is about a preference between Shi'a and Sunni. I think it is a very strong Russian preference for stability at any cost, almost.

And so they would rather not have extremist groups, certainly, something that they fear in their own periphery and even in their own federation. But they also have a strong preference just for stability, and both of these things lead to support for Assad.

There are other issues as well, but both of these things lead in the same direction.

Mr. SHERMAN. Dr. Takeyh, how bad is the economic situation in Iran now and if you could write one more sanctions law what would it be, and how dependent is Iran—I will give you a hint on the second question with my third—on spare parts from Europe and other American allies? If an elevator breaks down in a building in Tehran can they fix it without getting a part flown in from Germany?

Mr. TAKEYH. In terms of the economy, according to the IMF statistics, which they rely on—the Iranian Central Bank so who knows how reliable they are—IMF suggested Iran's economy is likely to grow by about 2 percent.

Mr. SHERMAN. That is better than our growth. And then can you also talk about the black market value of their currency because that is something the Iranians can't——

Mr. TAKEYH. Right. They had a liquidity crisis but I think they have managed it. They have taken the hits on that. It is a country that still relies a great deal on spare parts, as you suggested, but increasingly they are beginning to have deficient spare parts from China and other—developing alternative sources and alternative measures to get their economy going.

But it is very much still a stagnant economy in the sense that economic opportunities are having a difficult time keeping up with demographics.

Mr. SHERMAN. And if you could write one additional sanctions law that would cripple or at least hurt the Iranian economy over the next 5 years what would it be?

Mr. TAKEYH. Well, the key would be to essentially limit their export of oil and that they only have five or six customers now so that is going to be difficult to do with the Chinese but perhaps there is more leverage with the North Koreans and——

Mr. SHERMAN. Well, the real question here is not whether we are willing to have tens of thousands of Americans die on the ground, but whether we are willing to tell the Chinese that they have to choose between Iran and the United States as a business partner. The toughest adversary we may have in this is Wal-Mart.

Mr. TAKEYH. Right. I think it will be difficult to get Iranian exports down but that is where the soft spot is.

Mr. SHERMAN. Gotcha.

Mr. CHABOT. The gentleman's time has expired. The gentleman from Florida, Mr. DeSantis, is recognized for 5 minutes.

Mr. DESANTIS. Thank you, Mr. Chairman. Thank you, gentlemen, for your comments. Dr. Sachs, you had mentioned how the Israelis view the threat of a nuclear Iran and I think that you painted a picture that they were a little bit more accepting than maybe my understanding was going to be.

I mean, historian Bernard Lewis, one of the most knowledgeable historians of Islamic thinking, said that to people like Ali Khamenei and Ahmadinejad, the former President, mutually assured destruction is not a deterrent. It is an inducement for them because it serves to essentially hasten the messianic process, the return of the 12th Imam. So what kind of purchase does that have in Israeli thinking right now as they look at the threat?

Mr. SACHS. To clarify, I certainly do not mean to suggest that the Israeli Government views this in the way that I suggested. The Israeli Government's position is very clear that only zero enrichment—zero enriched uranium stock—only they are acceptable.

There are some very senior people from the center of the Israeli security establishment that view it in a slightly more nuanced way. They too though, again, don't think very differently from the Israeli administration. They simply think that if it was very low enrichment levels, and if the verification was very stringent, perhaps it would be liveable, perhaps it would be better than a situation with no agreement at all.

But, again, the differences are quite small in Israel. The rifts of opinion is quite small. On the issue of rationality, there is quite an interesting difference. Some suggest exactly as you quoted Bernard Lewis saying that the Islamic Republic is inherently irrational.

The prime minister of Israel has said this as well, and in that case they cannot be deterred by any of these means. But there are others, very central, in fact, in the cabinet itself, who have a slightly different view; who say that even the Soviet Union had—not messianic in the religious sense but messianic in the utopian sense—aspirations for the world and yet they could be deterred.

It is a very grim reality. It is not something we should hope for. The Cold War was certainly not a picnic but it may be more stable than the alternative.

Mr. DESANTIS. Yes, I would just say Iran's behavior to us is, clearly, irrational but if you accept some of the premises that the regime is based on—for example, Rafsanjani was quoted about a decade ago saying, Look, you know, we could wipe out 5 million Jews with one bomb and yes, we know that they would respond, and he is just doing this calculation kind of matter of factly.

And it probably would have killed 15 million Iranians but you know what? I mean, that is really an acceptable sacrifice. There are over 1 billion Muslims.

And so I think that some of the calculations that he made to us would, obviously, be irrational but if you believe in that apocalyptic view of Shi'ite Islam then it may be something and that is why I think it is so dangerous to allow Iran to develop a nuclear weapon. This is not like the Soviet Union, who was a very hostile regime.

At the end of the day they were atheist. If they got blown up there was nothing at the light at the end of the tunnel for them.

Let me ask you or I can—actually, any of the panelists. We have been talking about on this committee the role of ISIS in Iraq and what is happening there. I know Iran is involved. Quds Force is there.

I am trying to get a handle on exactly how involved they are. Would we see more Iranian involvement if, say, ISIS was threatening the Shi'ite holy sites?

I know they have talked about they wanted to actually destroy those. I take it that the Iranian regime would view that as a vital national interest of their country and that they may be willing to do even more than they have. What are the panelists' views on that?

Mr. MODELL. I think that they have already—that has already been in the front of their minds when they are trying to determine what is their calculus for involvement, figuring out the extent of their involvement in Iraq.

When they were looking at the—they were looking at the most important Shi'ite shrines and protecting them, that has been on their minds for a long time. I also think that you are going to see—if you start to see the ISIS moving further east and further south that you are going to continue to see a buildup of more regular Iranian forces.

Right now, they are relying considerably on proxies and the integration of those proxies into regular military—Iraqi military units and——

Mr. DESANTIS. You basically have the Shi'ite militia groups and then you have—there is a Quds Force commander, I think, and so you have the Quds Force with the kind of Sadrist militia groups that are the main source of kind of anti-ISIS opposition at this point?

Mr. MODELL. You have several different variations. You have—you have Shi'a militia groups fighting on their own. You have Shi'a militia groups that are partially integrated into Iraqi regular forces.

You have—and what you have, you know, IRGC Quds Forces officers overseeing those Shi'a militia groups in both roles and you have Shi'a militia groups integrating into Iraqi regular military uniforms. You have others where they are separated out.

You have stuff—you have joint units with the Kurds. I mean, the Iranians are doing everything they can to build up a large proxy force but then a lot of—it is a multifaceted effort.

Mr. DeSANTIS. Thank you. My time has expired. I would just say I think that we are running a very, very serious risk of walking into a bad deal here with the administration and what they have been doing and, you know, I think Congress really needs to speak out.

A bad deal will be worse than not having any deal at all, and I yield back the balance.

Mr. CHABOT. The gentleman's time has expired. The gentleman from Florida, Mr. Deutch, is recognized for 5 minutes.

Mr. DEUTCH. Thank you, Mr. Chairman. Thanks to the panelists. I would like to—I would like to take the conversation a little different direction.

There has been a lot of talk about the nuclear negotiations, what a deal looks like, how much leverage we have and what would happen if Iran—if there is no deal or if, looking ahead if Iran had a nuclear weapon, if they went to break out at the expiration of term or whatever the deal is, I would actually like to look at it differently.

What—if you could—if you could talk about what Iran's goals are with respect to its support for terror, what are its priorities and with respect to the nuclear deal we spend a lot of time talking about how dangerous these terrorist groups supported by Iran would be if Iran had nuclear weapons.

But what could Iran do with the immense amount of resources that it would possess if it struck a deal and foreign investment came pouring in, the economy turned around, its currency rebounded, inflation was—all the other things that would come from a deal for them, what could they do with that in their support of terror? Where would they focus and what would that mean for us?

Mr. TAKEYH. Historically, Iran's principal strategic arena of concern has been the Persian Gulf. So, in essence, you will see them, I think, with additional resources to be much more involved in Iraq and the Gulf States at the beginning level, and then there is that sort of organic attachment to Hezbollah and to a Palestinian rejectionist group—what there would be, essentially, in that sense.

The regime with additional resources would also have an opportunity to essentially legitimize itself domestically and perhaps craft an agreement with its population similar to the Chinese, namely, that in response to political acquiescence you get material rewards and vulgar nationalism.

So it might essentially have a new national compact with the population that could perhaps contribute to the regime's longevity.

Mr. DEUTCH. In other words, population says we can—we can live essentially—economically we can live Western lives. You do whatever it is you——

Mr. TAKEYH. Separate state from society.

Mr. DEUTCH. Dr. Sachs.

Mr. SACHS. In terms of what I said before, the Iranians do seem to be investing very heavily in Shi'a populations abroad.

Although they don't want to present themselves as leaders of the Shi'a, when in fact you look at where they invest their resources—their considerable resources—it tends to be there, probably because that is where they can find allies.

So you would expect that Lebanon, Syria—where not only Shi'a but other non-Sunni groups would have vast support, even bigger than they do today and that would be very considerable. In the Persian Gulf itself, one of the biggest concerns of Saudi Arabia is the fact that Saudi Arabia itself has a very sizeable Shi'a minority and in fact it is located just in the strategic area of where the oil is, and so this would be extremely dangerous, from their perspective.

Of course, Bahrain is Shi'a majority. From the Israeli perspective, Iranian activity already and even more so if it had more resources, is very low cost to Iran. Iran can fight Israel by proxy. It sends Hezbollah to do things. It arms PIJ and Hamas to do things. But Iran itself does not suffer the consequences and so it gains two things. First, it fights this holy war that it imagines, and the second is it gains a deterrent against Israel for any possible operation.

The debate I described earlier about Hezbollah, whether it will operate on the behest of Iran, is a very serious one from Israel thinking that if worst comes to worst and Israel has to act conventionally would Hezbollah get involved?

Some, at the beginning, thought maybe not and, as I said, the Syrian civil war just proved that of course they would—they would do so.

Mr. DEUTCH. I would just—I would like to narrow it down. So instead of talking about what Iran would do as the leader of the Shi'a around the world be specific. Which terrorist groups that it supports would it like to support more and what would those groups do with the resources?

Mr. TAKEYH. I would say certainly Hezbollah.

Mr. DEUTCH. Right.

Mr. TAKEYH. Hezbollah has already been a very generous beneficiary of Iran. After 2006 when Hezbollah misadventured into war the Iranians essentially helped rebuild much of its infrastructure.

So it would be—that would be different, and also various Shi'i militia groups that Iran would have to use in order to manipulate the politics of that country and potentially in Saudi Arabia.

It is important to recognize, and I know my time is short, in many Middle Eastern countries their internal populations are a national security threat. Saudi Arabia views its own citizens of Shi'i belief as a national security threat because they can make common cause with an external threat. So there is a lot of opportunity for mischief.

Mr. MODELL. I would agree with everything he said. The only thing I would add in terms of what specific groups would be—would be supported in the focus I think it would stay mainly within the region. But I would also say it is important to look at the ways in which Iran right now is actually doing some of that—preparing the ground work for that.

So when you look at Iraq, when you look at Iranian-supported forces, particularly proxy forces that it is using in Iraq, you have Bahrainian. You have Yemenis. You have Afghans. You have a number of others.

They have been cultivating these relationships for a long time. I think it would be an expansion of those relationships, particularly when they leave Iraq and they go back home. They are going back home and they have stronger foundations of power for the regime.

Mr. CHABOT. The gentleman's time has expired. The gentleman from Florida, Mr. Yoho, is recognized for 5 minutes.

Mr. YOHO. Thank you, Mr. Chairman. Thank you, gentlemen, for being here. How does Iran's involvement with Iraq in dealing with the conflict with the Islamic state, how does that affect our negotiation with the nuclear deal with Iraq—I mean, Iran?

Mr. TAKEYH. Well, at this particular point I don't think it has an impact on it in the sense that Supreme Leader said he doesn't want to negotiate with the United States on this issue and Secretary Hagel has said the same thing.

I think both parties are trying to keep this segregated from the larger regional conflict that they have.

Mr. YOHO. Mr. Modell. Okay. Same.

All right. You know, the purpose of this negotiation or our sanctions up to this point was to prevent Iran from having a nuclear weapon.

Sitting in this room right here we have had meeting after meeting after meeting that says Iran is going to get a nuclear weapon. I mean, 6 to 8 months—we had meetings they said they are 6 to 8 months from having four to five nuclear weapons.

That was a year ago. So I can only assume with the experts sitting here they told us the truth so we should assume they probably have that. Yet the sanctions that we had didn't prevent that.

So can we realistically think that new sanctions or new negotiations are going to prevent Iran from having nuclear weapons, especially if there is a sunset clause? The reports I have read that said it is going to be 3 to 5 years from now—when those phase away is what Iran wants.

I mean, are we going to prevent them from ever having a nuclear weapon?

Mr. TAKEYH. Well, I would say in the aftermath of expirational sunset clause and I think their 5+1 including United States would like to have the longest sunset clause, maybe a decade.

After that, Iran has a right as any other NPT member to have an industrial-sized nuclear program similar to Japan's and that essentially gives it the ability to manufacture a large arsenal of nuclear weapons on short notice.

Mr. YOHO. Okay. So if we are going in that direction would it not be better for us to prepare for that and the rest of the world to prepare for that instead of wasting all this time trying to prevent something that they are going to do regardless if there is an agreement or not?

Because they have shown that they are not trustworthy and they are going to do this anyway so why don't we prepare for that and prepare the rest of the world to negotiate conditions on how another nation acts toward another? And I know we have treaty after treaty after treaty but yet that day is coming and I think it would behoove us to focus on that.

Mr. TAKEYH. I think that is right. I am not quite sure if it is inevitable for Iran to get nuclear weapons because I think there are things that can happen between now and then.

But I do think one of the reasons why we embrace negotiations and the negotiating process is because we don't want to ask the questions that you are asking—what if this issue is not susceptible to diplomatic mediation—and once you answer that question what does the after look like.

Mr. YOHO. Well, that is just it. It is like—but yet somebody has got to tell the emperor he doesn't have any clothes on. I mean, we all see it. We see it coming.

So I think it would behoove us as a nation and this—I want to bring this up because the subject of this meeting is "Iran's Destabilizing Role in the Middle East."

How is our foreign policy viewed? I mean, we have had Ambassadors in from all kinds of Middle Eastern countries in the last 2 weeks. They said the view of America is at the lowest point they have ever seen.

Our credibility is gone. They don't know what we stand for. It is like we have a compass like Jack Sparrow in "Pirates of the Caribbean."

It has got a broken compass and they don't know what our policies stand for. Our credibility has been lost and you, Dr. Sachs, you were talking about—you said the other parts of the world view us as weak.

Explain that. Is that militarily? Is that our foreign policy or is that the direction or the will to stand up and do what we view is right?

Mr. SACHS. I think in part it is a pendulum. I think it is very strong in the Middle East, perhaps stronger than elsewhere. But I think in the Middle East, in particular, it is a bit of a pendulum.

After the years of the previous administration, where there was a very involved U.S. policy with boots on the ground in massive numbers, we have seems to have swung in the other direction and the reaction in the Middle East has been severe.

It has been one that America has seemingly lost its resolve. They have taken the declinist literature seriously, which is a mistake, I think. And the result, of course, is that they now view the United States as not as resolved as it was in the past.

I would just add one point about the possibility of what we might do with an international coalition. Sustaining the sanctions, which the Congress has been very important in installing, this demands also cooperation with the coalition and to keep this coalition going there is some utility in these negotiations, even above and beyond the possibility of what a deal might bring.

Mr. YOHO. Right. But yet to have effective sanctions you are going to have to tell China what to do and we are not going to be able to do that, and as far as boots on the ground the only place I want our military's boots on the ground is in the United States of America.

And I would like at some point for you guys if you could submit a reset of our foreign policy of what you think we should be doing in America as far as dealing with the rest of the world because what we have done over the last 30 or 40 years it ain't working real well. Thank you.

Mr. CHABOT. The gentleman's time has expired and I would just note for the record this is my 18th year in Congress and I think that is the first time that I have heard a pirate Jack Sparrow referred to in the Foreign Affairs Committee.

So we appreciate Mr. Yoho for injecting that, and I think our final questioner this afternoon will be the gentleman from Florida, Mr. Vargas, is recognized for 5 minutes.

Mr. VARGAS. California.

Mr. CHABOT. My bad. California.

Mr. VARGAS. Mr. Chairman, that is okay but I love California. Just want to make sure it didn't get confused with Florida. I love Florida too.

I guess I would say this. I hope it is not inevitable that Iran would get nuclear weapons because, unfortunately, I think that they would use them.

I mean, I think it is one of those regimes that would be willing to do that. I have been very sceptical of this interim agreement. I think it was a bad deal. I continue to think it is a bad deal because of naivete on our side.

I am even more sceptical of a long-term agreement if it is not a permanent agreement and the reason for that is I remember 1970. I am old enough to remember that and the hostage taking.

That was 35 years ago. I mean, certainly, I think the Iranians will wait us out if it is only 7 or 10 years and they will have the ability then to break out and have a nuclear weapon and I think that they would use that in many different ways.

Even if they didn't use the weapon itself, which I think they probably would, they would use it at least to destabilize the area.

And so I look at this very sceptically. I did think that the sanctions program was working. I think what we did here in this House was the appropriate thing and that was to ratchet them down.

And then if were going to get to an agreement I think the agreement had to be this: Either you do away with your nuclear program completely—no enrichment, no ability to create a nuclear weapon—or we continue down this path of sanctions and you have no economy and you probably lose your regime.

Make them decide that first. Then you can back up and do the interim agreements. We didn't do that, unfortunately, and so I think we are in a very difficult situation.

So now what do we do? I mean, we are in this situation now. I think that it is a very dangerous one. What do we do? I mean, you are the experts. What should we do?

Mr. TAKEYH. I would say in the next—given the fact that our course of leverage has not been sufficient to compel Iranian compliance, I think it is time for Congress and the White House to sort of come together on what they want to see in terms of another sanctions bill.

The White House would have its preferences and equities and the Congress would have. But I think it is time for the two branches of government to come together.

If our leverage has not been sufficient to get Iranian compliance in the last 6 months, why do we think it is going to be sufficient to get Iranian agreement in the next 6 months unless we do something different? So that is what I would argue.

Mr. VARGAS. How about yourself, Mr. Modell?

Mr. MODELL. The only thing I would add, I think the only reason Iran has come to the negotiating table—I mean, this is a point that has been stressed over and over—is out of economic necessity and it is because we had a strong position on the sanctions that this Congress put forth were as strong as they have ever been.

It is fantastic. I agree with Dr. Takeyh's guidance that the administration—there has to be better collaboration on this between this administration and the Congress on figuring out the way forward.

The last thing I would do is make sure that we shore up allied support on, you know, from the European Union in particular on oil sanctions and other things before we lose them.

Mr. VARGAS. Thank you. Dr. Sachs.

Mr. SACHS. Finally, just on this point, I think to maintain the sanctions, to maintain cooperation from our allies, it is crucial that if these talks fail, whether this week or in 6 months, that Iran is blamed—that Iran is blamed in the eyes of others and not the United States.

And this entails from us to be slightly more pragmatic in the short term but keeping our eye on the long game, and to do that we need to make sure—we need to understand, I think, that the key to keeping this pressure on Iran is actually our alliance with the other P5+1 countries and the EU in particular. And to do that we will have to be creative about how we approach this problem.

Mr. VARGAS. And I guess I would say this. You know, we always talk in sort of obfuscating terms. We always say keep all the options on the table.

Mr. Modell, you kind of broke that taboo today and you actually talked about using conventional force, and I would like to talk just a second about that because I think that there is this huge hesitation even to think about that other than in this obscure sort of way of saying keep all options on the table.

But what—really what it looked like if we had to do something militarily? Let us talk about that for a second because I think that we should say what it is and that is not all options on the table but military action.

Mr. MODELL. I am not sure what the context was in which I said—that I said I would advocate the use of——

Mr. VARGAS. Not the advocation of it—the possibility of it. That might need to be what we do.

Mr. MODELL. No, actually I think that—listen, as long as the Supreme Leader thinks that that is possible I think it is going to compel him to actually take the fact that we are pushing on this nuclear issue seriously.

If he doesn't believe there is—that that threat even exists or is credible any longer I think he is going to start trying to figure out all the—go to fall back on all the sophisticated ways in which they, you know, relied on denial and deception and dissimulation for the last 35 years.

I personally agree that we need to go back to what you just suggested, which was a very strong sanctions position before anything else.

Mr. VARGAS. I agree. My time has expired. I thank you, Mr. Chairman.

Mr. CHABOT. Thank you very much and, again, my apologies for misidentifying the gentleman's state. I apologize.

Mr. VARGAS. No worries, sir.

Mr. CHABOT. So I think that concludes the questioners this afternoon so—this morning, rather. We—actually we are afternoon, and would like to thank the panel for their testimony.

All members will have 5 days to extend their remarks or submit written questions. If there is no further business to come before the committee we are adjourned.

Thank you.

[Whereupon, at 12:07 p.m., the committee was adjourned.]

APPENDIX

MATERIAL SUBMITTED FOR THE RECORD

FULL COMMITTEE HEARING NOTICE
COMMITTEE ON FOREIGN AFFAIRS
U.S. HOUSE OF REPRESENTATIVES
WASHINGTON, DC 20515-6128

Edward R. Royce (R-CA), Chairman

July 16, 2014

TO: MEMBERS OF THE COMMITTEE ON FOREIGN AFFAIRS

You are respectfully requested to attend an OPEN hearing of the Committee on Foreign Affairs, to be held in Room 2172 of the Rayburn House Office Building (and available live on the Committee website at http://www.ForeignAffairs.house.gov):

DATE: Wednesday, July 16, 2014

TIME: 10:00 a.m.

SUBJECT: Iran's Destabilizing Role in the Middle East

WITNESSES: Mr. Scott Modell
                          Senior Associate
                          Burke Chair in Strategy
                          Center for Strategic and International Studies

                          Ray Takeyh, Ph.D.
                          Senior Fellow for Middle Eastern Studies
                          Middle East Program
                          Council on Foreign Relations

                          Natan B. Sachs, Ph.D.
                          Fellow
                          Saban Center for Middle East Policy
                          The Brookings Institution

By Direction of the Chairman

The Committee on Foreign Affairs seeks to make its facilities accessible to persons with disabilities. If you are in need of special accommodations, please call 202/225-5021 at least four business days in advance of the event, whenever practicable. Questions with regard to special accommodations in general (including availability of Committee materials in alternative formats and assistive listening devices) may be directed to the Committee.

COMMITTEE ON FOREIGN AFFAIRS
MINUTES OF FULL COMMITTEE HEARING

Day __Wednesday__ Date _____07/16/14_____ Room_____2172_____

Starting Time _10:08 a.m._ Ending Time _12:07 p.m._

Recesses | _0_ | (____to ____) (____to ____) (____to ____) (____to ____) (____to ____) (____to ____)

Presiding Member(s)

Edward R. Royce, Chairman
Rep. Steve Chabot

Check all of the following that apply:

Open Session ✓
Executive (closed) Session ☐
Televised ✓

Electronically Recorded (taped) ✓
Stenographic Record ✓

TITLE OF HEARING:

Iran's Destabilizing Role in the Middle East

COMMITTEE MEMBERS PRESENT:

See Attendance Sheet.

NON-COMMITTEE MEMBERS PRESENT:

None

HEARING WITNESSES: Same as meeting notice attached? Yes ✓ No ☐
(If "no", please list below and include title, agency, department, or organization.)

STATEMENTS FOR THE RECORD: _(List any statements submitted for the record.)_

Rep. Connolly

TIME SCHEDULED TO RECONVENE _____
or
TIME ADJOURNED _12:07 p.m._

Edward Burrier, Deputy Staff Director

HOUSE COMMITTEE ON FOREIGN AFFAIRS
FULL COMMITTEE HEARING

PRESENT	MEMBER	PRESENT	MEMBER
X	Edward R. Royce, CA	X	Eliot L. Engel, NY
X	Christopher H. Smith, NJ		Eni F.H. Faleomavaega, AS
X	Ileana Ros-Lehtinen, FL	X	Brad Sherman, CA
X	Dana Rohrabacher, CA		Gregory W. Meeks, NY
X	Steve Chabot, OH	X	Albio Sires, NJ
	Joe Wilson, SC	X	Gerald E. Connolly, VA
	Michael T. McCaul, TX	X	Theodore E. Deutch, FL
	Ted Poe, TX	X	Brian Higgins, NY
	Matt Salmon, AZ	X	Karen Bass, CA
	Tom Marino, PA	X	William Keating, MA
	Jeff Duncan, SC	X	David Cicilline, RI
X	Adam Kinzinger, IL		Alan Grayson, FL
	Mo Brooks, AL	X	Juan Vargas, CA
X	Tom Cotton, AR	X	Bradley S. Schneider, IL
	Paul Cook, CA	X	Joseph P. Kennedy III, MA
X	George Holding, NC	X	Ami Bera, CA
	Randy K. Weber, Sr., TX	X	Alan S. Lowenthal, CA
X	Scott Perry, PA	X	Grace Meng, NY
X	Steve Stockman, TX	X	Lois Frankel, FL
X	Ron DeSantis, FL	X	Tulsi Gabbard, HI
X	Doug Collins, GA	X	Joaquin Castro, TX
	Mark Meadows, NC		
X	Ted S. Yoho, FL		
	Sean Duffy, WI		
	Curt Clawson, FL		

Statement for the Record
Submitted by the Honorable Gerald Connolly

Iran plays a destabilizing role in the Middle East to serve the Islamic Republic's broader goals for regional influence. The pursuit of a domestic nuclear program, provision of arms to Hamas in Gaza, the financing of Hezbollah in Lebanon, support for Bashar al-Assad in Syria and recruitment for Shia militias in Iraq are not disjointed actions taken by a mischievous regime. These actions are instead part of Iran's concerted effort to strengthen its regional presence and in most instances carried out to the detriment of the people of the Middle East and United States interests.

For decades, the U.S. has countered Iran's underhanded dealings in the Middle East with isolation and sanctions. The U.S. has designated Iran as a State Sponsor of Terrorism since 1984, banned non-humanitarian foreign aid and repeatedly condemned the human rights abuses committed against the country's ethnic and religious minorities. There have been a litany of measures passed during my tenure in Congress that establish and strengthen sanctions against the Islamic Republic, including H.R. 2194, the Comprehensive Iran Sanctions, Accountability, and Divestment Act (111th) and the subsequent H.R. 1905, Iran Threat Reduction Act (112th). The sanctions regime against Iran also includes a ban on arms sales, restrictions on international lending, and the prohibition of business with Iranian banks that have been named as proliferation or terrorism supporting entities. On July 10, I joined with 341 of my colleagues, including the Chairman and Ranking Member in sending a letter regarding the P5+1 negotiations to President Obama urging him to consult with Congress before relaxing any sanctions on Iran.

The P5+1 negotiations over Iran's domestic nuclear program are the first meaningful engagement the U.S. has had with Iran in over 30 years. There is cautious optimism that the talks will encourage Iran to reduce enrichment activities, dilute its current stockpile of nuclear material, and continue to work with the U.S. and our partners on a more comprehensive agreement to scale back Iran's nuclear program. The Joint Plan of Action finalized on November 24, 2013 established a July 20, 2014 deadline for the talks with the option for negotiators to pursue a six-month extension. Comments by Secretary Kerry in Vienna this week indicate that the Administration is currently weighing this option as it considers the progress that has been made thus far and the likelihood that a final agreement can be reached through the current negotiated framework.

I think many of my colleagues would agree that the issue of halting Iran's nuclear program should be a priority for this Administration, and I await further progress in the talks and the forthcoming consultation with Congress. However, one priority does not obscure the rest for a sophisticated operation such as the United States foreign policy apparatus. The U.S. has not turned a blind eye to the role Iran is playing in many of the region's flashpoints at the moment. Hamas receives shipments of arms from Iran with which it attacks our close ally Israel. Fortunately, the Iron Dome technology partly financed by the United States is providing some measure of protection to the Israeli people. However, the arms shipments from Iran only facilitate a vicious cycle of retaliation in the Gaza Strip and exacerbate tensions that threaten to galvanize support for further conflict.

While Iran and the U.S. share a common enemy in the terrorist organization, the Islamic State of Iraq and Syria (ISIS), Iran's support is predicated on its goals to further a Shiite-Sunni divide in Iraq and protect its closest ally in the region in the Assad regime in Syria. The end for Iran is hardly regional stability. It encouraged the purge of Sunnis from service in the Iraqi government and military that precipitated gains by ISIS in Iraq, and it continues its support for Assad despite international condemnation for his use of chemical weapons on his own people. The U.S. has placed advisors in Iraq to fortify Iraqi forces' training and readiness and made clear that further assistance will be conditional upon more inclusiveness in the Iraqi government. The U.S. has also provided more than $1 billion in humanitarian assistance to help address the human cost of the violence perpetrated by the Assad regime and its Iranian facilitators.

I look forward to hearing from our witnesses today on how the U.S. can continue to counter Iranian destabilization efforts. The interest for Iran in many of these conflicts is very narrow. I would hope that recommendations from our panel provide an appropriate counter to Iran and continue the United States' far-reaching goals of stability and democratization in the Middle East.

Questions for the Record
Submitted by the Honorable Alan Lowenthal
To Mr. Scott Modell

Question 1:

It seems highly unlikely that Israel will publicly support an Iranian nuclear deal. However, given the present reality of the JPA/(P5+1), what would be an acceptable agreement for Prime Minister Netanyahu and for the opposition parties?

Answer:

To Israel, there are no acceptable solutions under consideration at the moment. If Iran comes out with a deal that allows it to retain a domestic enrichment capacity, Israel will not support it. The key going forward will be a global containment apparatus that reassures Israel and other skeptics that breakout will be detected on time and effectively countered. There hasn't been much discussion of the particulars of that.

Question 2:

There have been some differences between HAMAS and Iran since they take different sides in Syria-Iran supports Assad, while HAMAS opposed him. If Israel invades Gaza, what will the Iranians do?

Answer:

Invasion already in motion. Iran will monitor closely, no direct involvement. Too busy in Iraq and Syria at the moment to divert additional resources, which are scarce already.